Kenneth Lo was born in Foochow, China, and was educated at the Universities of Peking, Cambridge and London. Since arriving in England in 1936 he has been a diplomat, publisher of Chinese prints, industrial relations officer (with Chinese seamen in Liverpool), lecturer, journalist, BBC broadcaster and professional tennis player.

But Kenneth Lo is best known today as one of the world's authorities on Chinese cooking. He has written numerous successful books on Chinese cookery, including *The Complete Chinese Cookbook*, also available in Fontana.

Apart from writing about Chinese food and managing one of London's top Chinese restaurants, Kenneth Lo now runs a very successful multi-region Chinese cookery school. During 1982–3 two television films were made of Kenneth Lo's activities: a six-part series by Thames Television on Chinese cooking *A Taste of China*, and a documentary film of his life by Central Independent Television.

However, the one activity that Kenneth Lo has pursued continuously throughout his life is tennis. He was a Chinese Davis Cup and Wimbledon player in 1946, and four decades later he was chosen to represent Great Britain in the Britannia Cup for Veterans and was selected to play again for Britain in the 1984 Crawford Cup for Super-veterans.

Kenneth Lo

New Chinese Vegetarian Cookery

This edition published 1996 by Diamond Books
77-85 Fulham Palace Road
Hammersmith
London W6 8JB

First published 1986 by Fontana Paperbacks

Printed in Great Britain

Contents

Contents

Introduction

The recent drift away from meat-eating and meat cookery towards vegetable-eating and vegetable cookery is becoming more and more apparent in the affluent West. This can be put down to the natural swing of the pendulum; the fact that too much importance was attached to meat-eating and cookery in the past, and too little to cooking and eating vegetables. Traditionally, vegetables have only been treated as a supplement to meat by the rich, while the poor, or peasants, could rarely afford to eat meat (except for the game they caught) and therefore had to survive on roots and vegetables. Now, an English friend of mine tells me, it is the wealthy who are turning vegetarian!

During the nineteenth and twentieth centuries, a period of unprecedented economic growth and expansion, the West – always in a hurry as a whole – never took the trouble to explore all the avenues of creative cookery. Whatever opportunity there may have been was wasted on harking back to the glorious Empire days of French cuisine, which concentrated on creating sauces to accompany meat and vegetables, rather than on developing the flavours of the meats and vegetables themselves. More recently, the mass production of beef, lamb and chicken in Australasia, the United States and Argentina has encouraged an excessive consumption of meat – another reason why the art of cooking vegetables has not been properly developed in the West.

It has only been in the last couple of decades that the West has become aware of, and begun to appreciate, the range of cookery traditions and practices which exists in the other continents of the world. Interest in ethnic cooking is currently booming, with Indian and Chinese cuisines probably being the most popular – and these are, of course, mainly vegetable and cereal based. This new interest also seems to have encouraged a fresh Western interest in vegetable cookery.

It is also true to say that the Western disillusionment with and loss of interest in meat has stemmed from the constant overuse of meat in the average meal, and from not allowing vegetables to be integrally incorporated into meat dishes. This limits the number of meat (or primarily meat) dishes which can be produced; but, in Chinese 'compound cookery', for example, where meats and vegetables *are* often incorporated together in the same dish, the number of dishes which can be created is truly unlimited. Hence with Chinese food and cooking there is as yet very little apparent drift from meat to vegetable cookery, partly because there is much more middle ground between meat and vegetable cookery in China; and partly because urbanization and industrialization are only very recent phenomena in China, and the country has not yet reached the standard of living where meat is eaten in such quantities that people have begun to get bored with it. On the contrary, over 90 per cent of the population in China still live off the land, and much of the time they live almost entirely on cereals and vegetables. Indeed, for the majority of Chinese, meat is only served occasionally in the average household, maybe no more than once a fortnight, or even once a month. The rest of the time they have had to make do with largely meatless meals, and look forward to a special occasion when a pig might be slaughtered or a chicken killed to celebrate a wedding, birthday, memorial, anniversary or festival. China today still strives towards the bulk of the population eating more meat of all types, rather than less.

Where Chinese cookery can contribute to the Western interest in vegetarian cooking lies primarily in its ability to draw upon the immense resources and cookery experience of the peasantry of China, which are largely vegetarian. Secondly, it draws upon the Buddhist influence on Chinese cookery, which is fairly prominent throughout all the different levels of Chinese society over the centuries. Vegetarianism in the past was largely centred around the Buddhist monasteries and temples. There were temples in most large villages or small townships, and monasteries of different sizes were dotted and scattered throughout all the provinces of China.

Although Buddhism is not, and never has been, a state religion in China, because it is inextricably involved with Confucianism and Taoism in the Chinese subconscious, and in the Chinese striving to find comfort, and an explanation for man's place in this universe, its influence is broader than its official establishments. Many Chinese practise Buddhism even if not officially affiliated to any Buddhist organization; and as a result, because the Chinese are partially Buddhist, they are also at least partially vegetarian. Since freedom of belief is enshrined in the Chinese constitution, and a majority of temples and monasteries are nowadays being vigorously restored to their former often-garish glory, I imagine much of Buddhism and its vegetarian practices have now survived the rigours of revolution and the devastation of the Cultural Revolution. Indeed, my feeling is that, in general, the Chinese Buddhist vegetarians cooking today are only just beginning to find their feet again, have had too little time to find any new bearing, and are mostly inclined to hark back to the past. Many of the exploitable territories are still waiting to be explored; like much of China's heritage as it comes into contact with the forward momentum of development which is taking place in the Western world.

Chinese cooking is likely to make the most contribution to Western vegetarian interest in the areas of culinary technique and the use of ingredients. Although the basic foods used in China – cereals and vegetables – are much the same as the familiar foods consumed in the West, the flavouring of ingredients and heating methods employed are derived from entirely different traditions. There should therefore be vast scope for adaptation and innovation using Chinese methods and ingredients to produce dishes which are acceptable and appealing to the average Western palate.

The principal methods of Chinese heating are those which the West is not completely familiar with. Methods that we Chinese use practically all the time are *steaming* and *stir-frying*. Soya-bean products and by-products are used extensively to flavour both vegetarian and other food, and we also use more ingredients which have been pickled, salted, dried and spiced to flavour in particular bulk foods than is customary in the West. In creating and generating taste, we rely more heavily on coating ingredients with hot flavoured and seasoned oil as a way of spreading the flavours from the stronger tasting foods to the neutral and blander foods, or to merge the seasoned and matured flavour with that of the sweet and fresh.

Furthermore, we are much more in the habit of 'cross-cooking' different ingredients which results not only in the greater blending of flavours but also of textures, colours and foods. Thus many more dishes can be created than would be possible if one were confined to simple cooking, as is the normal practice in the West. Chinese cross-cooking is achieved by cutting food materials into small pieces, whether into shreds, thin slices or diced cubes, which enables them to be stirred or tossed together at different temperatures with greater ease. A variety of sauces and different ingredients can be added as you go along for flavouring. Cross-cooking applies not only to different raw food materials but also to mixing well-cooked and seasoned ingredients with fresh uncooked food materials.

This practice of cross-cooking actually opens up innumerable avenues for the creative and enterprising chef. Although the Chinese chef is as equally bound by tradition and conventional practices as the classic Western chef, he is probably accorded a greater freedom of 'interpretation' because of the sheer complexity of Chinese cooking, and the numerous options opened to the chef at each stage of the cooking. This applies as much to vegetarian as to non-vegetarian cooking. Chinese recipes are seldom to be adhered to completely; they are written down more as guidelines for interested parties to follow and to make their own interpretations.

This brings us to the presentation of foods and dishes. Chinese cookery has a great advantage over *nouvelle cuisine*, which is bound to produce small, light dishes, and therefore project small postcard-size representations of the food they create and serve. The Chinese do not have such restrictions. Indeed, because Chinese dishes are usually created and cooked for half a dozen to a dozen people, the dishes are usually conceived on a much larger scale. Instead of always aiming to produce small-sized dishes, with their obvious limitations, the Chinese have a much freer rein. This can often lead to results comparable perhaps to landscape gardening, in which some parts of the 'garden' may be intricately and delicately designed in miniature, while other parts are allowed to grow wild. There is therefore much more scope for the practice of 'art to conceal art', resulting in more impressive effects. Consequently, Chinese cooking is likely to be much nearer to the ideals of *cuisine naturelle* than *nouvelle cuisine* in so far as it endeavours to project not only the appearance of natural foods, but also their natural flavours and characteristics. Nowadays these are often lost by the wayside through overzealous attempts to create man-made designs and to compress them into small spaces.

I should explain that what I am mostly concerned with in this book is not so much the classical vegetarian cuisine of China which often has its limitations. Traditionally, it is much too inclined to produce imitations of meat dishes, such as 'vegetarian duck', 'vegetarian goose', 'vegetarian fish' and so on, as if vegetables are only able to hold their ground if they achieve some semblance to meat. Indeed, there are instances where they have been successful in achieving a remarkable likeness to meat, for which they deserve our applause, but in endeavouring to do so they have sacrificed so much of their energy and creativeness, which could otherwise be devoted to bringing out the true assets and qualities of the vegetables themselves.

What I should like to do in this book is to bring about a renaissance of the vegetables themselves, in relation to the satisfaction and appeal which they can have for the human palate and other senses, whether through their flavour or their other essential qualities, such as texture, aroma, colour or shape, by applying to them the Chinese techniques of cutting, flavour-blending, heat control in cooking, and the use of supplementary materials and ingredients which are peculiar to Chinese cooking traditions. Some of these should help to add a new dimension to vegetarian food and vegetable cookery, which, whether they are practised in the East or West, are going through a period of considerable transformation.

In the past people have been content to imitate the classics. As more and more attention has been brought to bear on this, the past has often been found to be wanting. This has spurred many knowledgeable people on to explore new territories and make greater use of their own creative instincts. Few of us who have gained an acquaintance with the greatness of the classics are sufficiently satisfied to sit still and just worship the past. The world is always evolving and, whether in art, architecture or literature, every age must bring forth its new forms and concepts. Paintings did not stop with the French Impressionists, nor architecture with Wren and Capability Brown, nor literature with Dickens, Thackeray or the Lake poets, great though they may have been. Every artist who has any spark of creativeness is groping his or her way forward. Nowhere is this truer than in the world of cookery. With cookery publications nowadays overflowing the bookshelves, cookery writers and chefs all over the world must indeed be working overtime to break new ground. Yet, to find the means to initiate a 'culinary revolution', or at least to start a new trend, requires inspiration. It was said that the French were inspired by the daintier Oriental approach before embarking on their *nouvelle cuisine*. Within a very few years, however, they have realized the failings and limitations of this style of cooking in which excessive devotion to man-made designs and their visual effects were often achieved at the expense of flavour-blending and flavour generation. Western cooks, now being aware of this, and the staleness which they are experiencing from overdesigning without the corresponding development of flavour, are rapidly drifting away from *nouvelle cuisine* in search of pastures new, and could be heading towards *cuisine naturelle*. Whatever it is, it will require a degree of inspiration to point to new directions and put the next trend on course. Usually when the world's cooks are at a loss for inspiration, they revert back to their roots, which in France, for example, means going back to their 'bourgeois' cooking, their *cuisine paysanne*, their *cuisine régionale* and their established classics, which are, after all, the bulk and mainstay of their national culinary heritage.

In China today, because of the lapse in culinary development and interest suffered since the revolution of 1949, and especially during the decade of the Cultural Revolution of the 1960s, the country is making a conscious effort to catch up with the past. Innumerable cookery schools seem to have been established in every province in the country to speed up this process. Since the Chinese culinary heritage is a vast one, some time will elapse before they will feel the need to explore new ground. However, once the interest in food and cooking is rekindled, there are bound to be people who will experiment and find new ways of doing things. It is therefore likely that the 'new wave' in Chinese cooking will generate its first ripples and gradually gather momentum while it is still engaged in the process of catching up with the past.

During this period of innovation, Chinese cooking is likely to find its greatest inspiration to be from its contact with the West, coupled with the rediscovery of China's past and the vastness of its own resources. The influence of the West in culinary matters, as in all aspects of our activities, is likely to be felt all along the line. However, it should be pointed out that in cultural matters we Chinese have always regarded the

Western influence as something peripheral, rather than touching on the 'heart of the matter'. Considering the size, weight and vitality of the Chinese culinary heritage, it is likely that, although Western cookery methods may have a significant impact on Chinese cooking in the future, it should on the whole be able to maintain its completely independent character. In fact, Chinese cuisine should be able to contribute more to the world's culinary practices and culture at large than it is able to take and absorb from the West.

The situation with Chinese vegetarian cooking is similar; there is much which the Chinese have to do to rediscover their own heritage, and the West is likely to have an influence on the future of Chinese vegetarian food, and its preparation, during this period of rediscovery. Within China itself, as I have said, temples and monasteries are being renovated and rebuilt at some speed, and they will soon become centres of tourist interest once again – and the Mecca of Chinese vegetarian cooking at the same time. As this process gathers momentum, it should not take too long for the Chinese to reacquaint themselves with all their vegetarian classics.

It would be interesting to know the likely areas and directions in which Chinese vegetarian cooking is likely to develop from now on. As I see it, the one area in which it could profitably develop is to incorporate more fruits and flowers. This has arisen partly from the fact that some of the principal flavourings of Chinese food (vegetarian or otherwise) are soya based (that is, soya sauce, soya paste, bean 'cheese', and so on), and nearly all soya-based ingredients go together well with sugar or honey for their own savoury enrichment (a little-used practice in Western cuisine). Since the majority of fruits have a high sugar content, they should be capable of enhancing the richness and savouriness of vegetarian dishes when cooked together with vegetables and soya-based flavouring ingredients. Already in meat cookery, where more experimentation has been carried out than in vegetarian cooking, dishes such as beef and mango or shredded beef quick-fried with shredded pear have proved very successful, and these have both been cooked with soya-based marinades. There is no doubt that dates or dried figs can be further enriched by the application of a soya-based flavourer and cooked together with vegetables or pasta to produce delicious dishes. The use of cherries or sultanas in fried rice is an obvious example of how a fruit can be used in the context of a bulk food, together with salty pickles, to produce a dish of savoury rather than sweet appeal.

Chinese stir-fry cooking, where ingredients are cut into small or thin pieces and tossed and stirred together, offers great opportunities for mixing fruits, such as apples (fresh or dried), plums and peaches, with vegetables. Perfect specimens of the fruit can be left whole for decorative purposes to heighten the visual appeal. There are many instances where crunchy fruits can be used to vary and improve the textural interest of a dish, something which, up until now, was normally limited in Chinese cooking to water chestnuts and bamboo shoots.

Using flowers in Chinese cooking has long been a tradition. A typical dish is the well-known chrysanthemum hotpot, which gets its name partly from using chrysanthemum petals to garnish the top of the hot pot when serving, and partly from the shape of the flame which rises and caresses the pot from underneath like a large bloom of flaming chrysanthemums. All kinds of flower petals (such as violets, marigolds, nasturtiums and roses) can be added to Chinese stir-fried dishes. Some selected blooms of flowers can of course be left whole and perfect to add to the beauty of the dish. The peony, which is the Chinese national flower, is particularly effective because of its large and sturdy bloom. When bonsai miniature trees are featured together with flower-enhanced and decorated dishes we shall be entering a new dimension in food presentation. As long as we do not forget the importance of flavouring, and that the flavours of flowers are subtle and can easily be blotted out by the much stronger flavours of spices and herbs, we shall not reach the stage where aesthetic effects are achieved at the expense of culinary satisfaction. We must always try to remember that food is above all for the eating!

Those of us who are involved in cookery are deeply aware that all national cuisines are in need of breaking new ground, if they are to keep vibrant and alive. I feel that, not least of all, this applies to the cooking of China. I hope that I will be able to encourage you, too, to be adventurous and to try experimenting on the basis of some of my recipes.

Kenneth Lo, June 1985

1 Soya beans

One of the most remarkable qualities of soya beans is that it is not only one of the most nutritious foods but it is also self-flavouring. This has made soya sauce one of the principal flavouring agents for foods worldwide, and it is increasingly being used and accepted in the West. When ground soya beans are fermented together with flour and salt, subjected to the action of the sun, and a variety of strong-tasting vegetables added, they are capable of producing a whole range of soya-based products and by-products, which can be used not only in cooking, but also as condiments on the table. Gourmets in China can often be heard talking about soya sauce and soya pastes with all their varieties of flavour, thickness or strength in the same knowing manner as the Western connoisseurs talk about wines, with their vintages, maturities, fruitiness, full-bodiedness, and so on. It is not just a matter of thick, dark soya sauce, or light soya sauce (which would be like grading wine as just red or white).

In Japan they have been eating tofu and using mesos for flavouring for many hundreds of years, but that to the Chinese is no more than scratching the surface. Soya sauce and soya pastes were already being manufactured in China during the millennium before Christ, or before the first emperor of China, Tsing Shi Huang Di. It is interesting to note that these soya products were not made in factories but in 'soya gardens' (*jiang yuan*). Presumably, even in those far-off days, soya sauce and soya pastes were made in much the same manner as they are largely made today. Soya beans and flour ferment in brine in large, widemouthed earthen jars which are lined up on the ground in a walled garden. The wide mouth of the jars facilitates the action of the sun, and the gradual evaporation of the brine, so that the eventual product can be adjusted to different degrees of thickness. Apparently, the Chinese started to use soya-bean products even before they had discovered the benefit of 'stir-fry' cooking. Before the days of stir-frying, soya products were simply added into meat and vegetable stews which were cooked in a large cauldron called *ding*, together with cereals. With the advent of stir-frying a special form of cooking called *bao* was developed. Meat or root vegetables (or both) are lightly cooked and put to one side. Soya sauce or soya paste is mixed with stock, sugar, wine and chopped strong-tasting vegetables in a wok or frying pan, and reduced to a creamy sauce. The meat or vegetables are returned to the pan or wok for a rapid turn and second cooking in the bubbling sauce. This method of cooking is still widespread in China today, especially in the north.

One of the most popular forms of Chinese cooking is *shao* which simply involves stewing your ingredients in stock with soya sauce, soya paste and sugar added. For more refined cooking, some wine is also added. In China stewing with soya sauce added is called 'red cooking', and since most foods can be cooked in this manner the number of dishes produced by red cooking is countless. This includes practically all poultry, meats and fish, as well as most vegetables. Red cooking is particularly suitable for most root vegetables, and the harder vegetables, such as carrots, aubergines, bamboo shoots, turnips, broccoli, cauliflower and asparagus stems, lotus roots, parsnips, brussels sprouts, celery, and the harder varieties of cabbage. A whole range of Chinese pickles comes into full play to enhance or vary the flavour when red cooking these vegetables, and in most instances bean curd in its usual form, or dried in the form of skins, sheets and strips of dried bean curd, is added to augment the dishes or vary their texture.

Cooking or stewing without the use of soya sauce is termed 'white cooking'. The harder vegetables are cooked and stewed in vegetarian stock, with 'bean curd cheese' added to achieve the same richness of flavour. In some instances, the stock and sauces (and dissolved 'cheese') are rapidly reduced over high heat to form a mere gloss or coating on the vegetables, which makes the dish extremely tasty. This form of cooking is called *kan shao* or 'dry stewed'. Ordinary bean curd may be added, or more often dried bean curd strips, or rehydrated bean curd skins, to cook together with the other vegetable ingredients to produce dishes with typical Chinese feel and flavour. In most of these dishes a few drops of sesame oil may be added during the very last stage of the cooking to enhance their aromatic appeal.

As can be seen clearly from above, even if we were to confine ourselves to a few methods of cooking, such as red or white cooking, and dry stewing, a considerable range of dishes can be produced without leaving the doorstep of the soya-bean family. If we were also to indulge in other forms of much-used Chinese cooking such as stir-frying and steaming, as well as several dozen other different but accepted and well-established methods, an even greater number of dishes can be charted and cooked. What is intriguing about Chinese cooking is that whenever a new method of cooking is introduced and adopted, it immediately opens up fresh avenues, along which a vast number of dishes can be created, by varying the permutation of ingredients. What is remarkable about soya-bean products and by-products is that somewhere within this permutation they can usually be put to use either as a principal bulk food or as a savoury agent. Since the majority of Chinese dishes aim to produce a balance of the light, bland, natural flavour with that of the strong spicy and mature flavour, soya beans, their products and by-products are almost invariably called in to play their part in one form or another, whether in vegetarian or non-vegetarian cooking. The importance of soya products, especially in the form of bean curd or soya sauce, in Chinese cooking can hardly be overestimated.

Soya sauce and other soya-based seasoning and flavouring agents are rarely domestically made in China; they are readily available and almost invariably bought. Bean curd or tofu is also usually bought, but it can be made quite easily at home, with the help of a blender. If immersed in water and stored in the refrigerator, it keeps quite well for a week. One of the simplest ways to make bean curd or tofu is as follows.

Bean Curd (or Tofu) Dishes

Bean Curd or Tofu

Wash and rinse soya beans in water (1 cup of beans to 1½ cups of water) and grind into a purée. Bring the purée to the boil in a large pan, and simmer gently for 15–20 minutes.

Separate the solid in the purée from the soya milk by straining the cooked purée through a piece of muslin or cheesecloth placed in a large colander. This soya milk so obtained is what is used for making bean curd or tofu in China. The soya milk is augmented by pouring cold water into the purée and straining the liquid into the soya milk. The soya mash or pulp (called *okara* in Japan) left in the muslin or cheesecloth, which is also nutritious, should be reserved for a different purpose.

The soya milk should now be transferred to a large saucepan, brought quickly to the boil and removed from heat.

Now stir in the 'coagulant' to curdle the 'milk'. The coagulant may consist simply of vinegar or lemon juice; gypsum (calcium sulphate); Epsom salts (magnesium sulphate); or one of the Japanese natural solidifiers called Nigari, which is often available from oriental food stores. The coagulant is usually dissolved first in water, and then stirred into the soya milk in two to three stages. Leave 4–5 minutes between each addition of the coagulant. When the soya milk has curdled and the liquid is clear – no longer milky – no more coagulant need be added.

The curdled soya milk is then poured into a specially designed, square or oblong perforated wooden box, lined with cloth or muslin, which allows the curdled 'milk' to separate and flow out into the container. The liquid should be reserved for other uses. Allow time for as much of this clear liquid to be strained away from the curdled curd as possible.

When this is done, fold the sides of the cloth over the top of the curd in the lined wooden box, which forms the square or oblong shape of the bean curd. A flat wooden lid of the same shape, but slightly smaller, which fits inside the top of the box, is then placed on top of the coagulated curd to press it down. A small weight (1–1.15 kg/2–3 lb) is then placed on top of the lid to provide additional pressure. After 30–45 minutes, when all the liquid has been pressed out of it, the bean curd should be ready for use. The heavier the weight used, the firmer the bean curd will be.

Since the bean curd is made in a square or oblong box it comes out in these shapes. It can be cut into halves or quarters or into any convenient sizes and shapes . . .

To keep bean curd, it should be completely immersed in water. If kept for more than one day, the water should be changed once a day, or every other day. If put in a refrigerator, it should keep in good condition for 5–6 days.

Both by-products derived from making bean curd – soya milk (*tou-jiang*) and soya mash (*tou-ja*) – can be used quite independently of bean curd. Soya milk is widely drunk as milk, and soya mash is used for cooking rougher dishes; can be combined with other cereals to make bread and pasta; added to meats to make it go further, being much cheaper and just as nutritious; and used as poultry and animal feed.

Once you embark on tofu cookery, you are entering a world of its own. Given the wide variety of Chinese cooking methods, and the influence of Western cookery with its whole range of dairy produce, the number of dishes which can be created using tofu either as the main or as the supplementary ingredient is simply limitless.

Bean Curd Salad or Chinese Cold-tossed Bean Curd

Since bean curd has already been cooked, it can be served cold without any further cooking or heating. Hence it is a favourite food for serving cold as an hors d'oeuvre with hot rice-porridge (*congee*). Since the Chinese palate leans towards savouriness, to contrast with the blandness of plain cooked rice (whether in the form of porridgy rice eaten at breakfast time, or the drier, steamed or boiled rice eaten at other meals), bean curd is usually tossed together with some pronounced-tasting ingredients (such as chopped pickle), or salty ingredients and spicy sauces when served as an hors d'oeuvre or in cold-tossed salads. For palates which are used to vegetarian food, such hors d'oeuvres are appealing both because of the subtle and satisfying flavour of 'raw' bean curd, and the sharp, tasty impact of the flavouring ingredients and sauces applied. Although the appreciation of such bean curd dishes is a cultivated one, this can quite easily be acquired, and once acquired the palate will always have a yearning for its combined simplicity and subtlety. Both the Chinese and Japanese will go a long way to have an uncomplicated bean curd hors d'oeuvre or salad, and these are usually served to start a meal, or as one of several dishes served to complement the rice during any Chinese meal.

Cold-tossed Bean Curd with Sesame or Peanut Butter Sauce
Serve with hot cooked rice, or rice-porridge (*congee*) along with 2–3 or more accompanying dishes.
Serves 4, with rice

3–4 cakes bean curd	1 tbs vegetable oil
Dressing:	¾ tbs sesame oil
2 tbs sesame paste or peanut butter	2½ tbs light soya sauce
	1½ tbs malt vinegar

Drain the bean curd, and cut each piece into quarters. Spread them on a serving dish. Mix the sesame paste or peanut butter with sesame oil and vegetable oil until well blended. Mix the soya sauce with vinegar. Place a large dollop of the sesame paste or peanut butter on top of each piece of bean curd. Pour an appropriate amount of the soya-sauce-vinegar mixture over them.

Cold-tossed Bean Curd with Chinese Pickles

Serve with hot cooked rice, or rice-porridge (*congee*) along with 2–3 or more accompanying dishes.
Serves 4, with rice and other dishes

4 cakes bean curd	1½ tbs vegetable oil
Dressing:	1 tbs sesame oil
1½ tbs Sichuan Ja Tsai (hot) pickle	2½ tbs light soya sauce
1½ tbs Tientsin snow pickle (salty and sour)	1 tbs malt vinegar

Chop the two pickles into a medium-fine mince, and mix them together. Blend the oils together, and then the soya sauce and vinegar together. Cut the cakes of bean curd into quarters.

Drain and spread the bean curd pieces on a serving dish. Sprinkle an appropriate amount of chopped pickle and the soya-sauce-vinegar mixture over each. Finally, drip a large drop or two of mixed oil over each piece of bean curd.

Hot-tossed Bean Curd in Spring Onion and Coriander Sauce

This dish will particularly appeal to anyone who likes the fragrance of coriander and the aroma of freshly chopped spring onion.
Serves 4, with rice and other dishes

4 cakes bean curd	3–4 tbs chopped spring onion
Hot Dressing:	2½ tbs light soya sauce
3 tbs vegetable oil (peanut or corn)	¾ tbs chilli sauce
1 tbs finely chopped root-ginger	2 tbs vegetarian stock
1 tbs finely chopped Sichuan Ja Tsai pickle	1 tbs dry sherry
3–4 tbs chopped fresh coriander leaves	1½ tsp sugar

Cut each piece of bean curd into four pieces. Poach them in boiling water for 1 minute. Lift them out with a perforated spoon, drain and place them on a serving dish.

Heat oil in a small frying pan or wok. When hot, add the ginger and pickle. Stir them around for ¼ minute. Add the coriander and spring onion. Stir them all around for ¾ minute, over medium heat. Add the soya sauce, chilli sauce, stock, sherry and sugar. Continue to stir all the ingredients together for a further ½ minute.

Pour the sauce and the ingredients in the frying pan or wok evenly over the bean curd in the serving dish. Serve immediately.

Bean Curd with Spinach and Radish

The contrast between the dark green of the spinach, the bright red and pink of the radish, and the whiteness of the bean curd makes for an attractive colour combination. Although simple to prepare, the flavour of each individual ingredient seems to be able to stand out distinctly. An excellent dish to serve as an hors d'oeuvre.
Serves 4–6

2 cakes bean curd	1½ tsp sugar
225 g (8 oz) radish (must be bright in colour)	2 tsp light soya sauce
	1½ tbs vegetable oil
3 tsp salt	½ tbs sesame oil
350 g (12 oz) young spinach	

Cut bean curd into large sugar-lump-sized cubes. Drain well. Top and tail each radish. Give each radish a heavy bash with the side of a chopper, or a rolling pin. Sprinkle and rub evenly with 2 tsp salt, and leave to season for half an hour.

Poach the spinach in a large pan of boiling water for ½ minute. Drain thoroughly, and squeeze as dry as possible. Place on a chopping board, and chop into rough mince. Place the minced spinach in a large basin. Add remaining salt, sugar, soya sauce, vegetable oil and sesame oil. Turn and toss them together well, and loosen them up. Add the bean curd cubes, and toss them lightly with the spinach, so that they are evenly mixed.

Spread the mixed bean curd and spinach evenly over a large serving dish in one layer. Drain away the excess water from the seasoned radishes and dot them evenly over the bean curd and spinach.

Bean Curd Salad with Chinese Salt Eggs
This dish makes an excellent summer starter.
Serves 4 (or more with rice and other dishes)

2–3 cakes bean curd	*Dressing*:
1 fresh cos lettuce	2 tbs light soya sauce
3 medium tomatoes	1½ tbs malt or wine vinegar
1 bundle watercress	1½ tbs salad oil
2 Chinese salt eggs (duck eggs, see page 49)	¾ tbs sesame oil
1½ tbs Sichuan hot pickle (Ja Tsai)	

Cut bean curd into large sugar-lump-sized pieces. Chop the lettuce into two or three pieces, and the tomatoes into eighths. Roughly chop the watercress and salt eggs and finely mince the pickle.

Lay the lettuce leaves evenly over a serving dish. Spread the tomato and watercress on top. Spread the bean curd cubes on top of the vegetables. Mix together the dressing ingredients, and drip the mixture over the bean curd and vegetables. Sprinkle the chopped pickle and salt egg over them.

Bean Curd Salad with Bean Sprouts and Hundred-year-old Eggs
Another excellent summer starter for any Chinese meal.
Serves 4 (or more with rice and other dishes)

Repeat the previous recipe using ¼ lb bean sprouts instead of watercress, and adding 2 hundred-year-old eggs (see page 50). These eggs should be thoroughly washed (they are normally sold encrusted in mud), shelled and cut into eight equal-sized segments. These segments should then be placed evenly on top of the vegetable salad, before they are sprinkled with chopped salt egg, pickle and the dressing.

Bean Curd with Tomato and Spring Onion

We Chinese are used to combining sweet-tasting dishes with savoury dishes, especially as a starter or side dish. Sliced tomato sprinkled with sugar is very frequently served in Peking in the summer.

Serves 4, with rice and other dishes

4–5 large, firm tomatoes	*Dressing:*
1½ tbs castor sugar	1½ tbs light soya sauce
2–3 cakes bean curd	1 tbs salad oil
2½ tbs chopped spring onion	½ tbs sesame oil

Cut each tomato into flat slices and spread them in one layer on top of a serving dish. Sprinkle sugar on top of each piece of tomato. Cut the bean curd into 8–12 cubes, and place these on top of the tomatoes. Sprinkle them with chopped spring onion. Mix together the ingredients for the dressing, and sprinkle evenly over the bean curd and tomatoes.

Carrot and Cucumber Salad with Bean Curd in Hot Soya Dressing

A good starter for a Chinese meal, in summer or winter.
Serves 4 (or more with rice and other dishes)

2 cakes bean curd	15-cm (6-inch) section
150–175 g (5–6 oz) young carrots	cucumber
½ tbs salt	

Hot Dressing:	3 tbs vegetarian stock
2 chillies	½ tsp salt
3 slices root-ginger, shredded	2 tsp chilli sauce
2½ tbs vegetable oil	1 tbs malt vinegar
2 tbs light soya sauce	¾ tbs sesame oil

Cut bean curd into large sugar-lump-sized cubes. Clean and scrape carrots under running water, then cut them slantwise at 5-mm (¼-inch) intervals into diagonal sections. Parboil them for 5 minutes. Drain them thoroughly and sprinkle and rub them with salt. Leave them to season for 1½ hours, and then drain away the extracted water and salt. Cut cucumber (including the skin) into similar, though larger, diagonal sections. Top and tail the chillies, and remove the pips.

Fry the chilli and ginger in a small pan or wok in hot oil over medium heat for 1¾ minutes. Add soya sauce, stock, salt, and chilli sauce. Stir-fry them together for ¾ minute. Remove from heat and stir in the vinegar and sesame oil. Toss together the carrots, cucumber and bean curd pieces in a bowl or deep-sided dish. Sprinkle and pour the dressing evenly over them.

Cold-tossed Bean Curd with Onion, Ginger and Spring Onion Dressing

The strong flavours of cooked onion and fresh spring onion make the bean curd remarkably appealing if you like the taste of onion.
Serves 4 (or more with rice and other dishes)

3–4 cakes bean curd	3 tbs vegetarian stock
1 small onion	1½ tbs dry sherry
3 slices root-ginger	1 tbs wine vinegar
3 tbs vegetable oil	3 tbs finely chopped spring
2 tbs light soya sauce	onion
2 tsp red bean curd 'cheese'	2 tsp sesame oil
¼ tsp freshly ground black	
pepper	

Cut each piece of bean curd into four pieces. Coarsely chop the small onion and finely chop the ginger.

Heat oil in a small pan or wok. When hot, add ginger and onion. Stir them in the hot oil for 1 minute over medium heat. Add soya sauce, bean curd 'cheese', pepper, stock, sherry and vinegar. Continue to stir the ingredients together for 1 minute.

Spread the bean curd pieces over a serving dish. Pour a drip of the dressing on top of each piece of bean curd, and place a large pinch of freshly chopped spring onion on top. Sprinkle them with sesame oil.

Cold-tossed Bean Curd with Egg and Garlic-ginger Dressing and Mixed Sauces

The contrast of flavour between the egg, dressing and bean curd seems to bring out the subtlety of the fresh flavour of the bean curd.
Serves 4 (or more with rice and other dishes)

4 cakes bean curd
3 hardboiled eggs
2 cloves garlic
2 slices root-ginger
1 tsp salt
¾ tsp pepper
2 tbs light soya sauce

1½ tbs hoisin sauce
2 tsp chilli sauce
1½ tbs vegetarian stock
1 tbs dry sherry
1½ tbs vegetable oil
½ tbs sesame oil

Cut each piece of bean curd into four. Chop eggs into small pieces. Crush garlic, and finely chop with the ginger. Mash them in with the eggs, adding salt and pepper. Mix soya sauce, hoisin sauce, chilli sauce, stock, sherry, vegetable and sesame oil together into a dressing.

Spread the bean curd over a serving dish. Add the seasoned egg and toss together lightly. Sprinkle the dressing mixture evenly over them.

Cold-tossed Bean Curd with Soya Egg, Spinach and Mustard Dressing
Serves 4 (or more with rice and other dishes)

3 cakes bean curd
6 tbs dark soya sauce
3 hardboiled eggs
225 g (8 oz) young spinach
1½ clove garlic

2 slices root-ginger
½ tsp salt
1½ tbs vegetable oil
1½ tsp sesame oil

Dressing:
1 tbs mustard powder
2 tbs water

2 tbs light soya sauce
1 tbs wine vinegar
1 tbs dry sherry

Cut each piece of bean curd into eight pieces. Heat soya sauce in a small saucepan. Add the boiled eggs to heat slowly in the soya sauce, turning them over all the time, until the eggs have taken on the dark brown colour of the sauce (about 4–5 minutes). Remove from heat. When cool, cut each egg into six equal segments.

Poach the spinach in boiling water for 1 minute. Drain thoroughly, pile it up and chop through it at 1-cm (½-inch) intervals. Crush the garlic, and chop and mince it together with ginger. Mix the garlic, ginger, salt, vegetable and sesame oil into the spinach. Turn and toss them together until well mixed.

Mix the dressing ingredients together until well blended. Spread the spinach as a bed on a serving dish. Place the soya egg segments and four bean curd pieces on top, well spaced out over the spinach. Sprinkle the dressing mixture evenly over them.

Cold-tossed Bean Curd with Chinese Pickle and Marinade

The difference between the sharpness of the taste and softness of flavour of the pickles and marinated ingredients, and their different textures, alongside the fresh blandness of the bean curd, seem to make the qualities of the latter stand out more pronouncedly.
Serves 4 (or more with rice and other dishes)

4 cakes bean curd	2 tbs chopped hot Sichuan Ja Tsai pickle
100–150 g (4–5 oz) tinned Chinese marinated bamboo shoots	1½ tbs chopped green snow pickle
6 medium-sized Chinese dried black mushrooms	1½ tbs chopped Tientsin savoury winter pickle
2 tbs dark soya sauce	2 tbs light soya sauce
1½ tbs dry sherry	¾ tbs sesame oil

Cut each piece of bean curd into 8–10 cubes. Cut the bamboo shoots into slices approximately 1–2 cm (½–¾ inch) thick (if they are not already sliced). Soak mushrooms in hot water for half an hour to soften. Remove stems, squeeze to dry and cut caps into quarters. Soak them in dark soya sauce and dry sherry for 30 minutes.

Place all the ingredients in a large bowl, and toss them lightly together. Turn them out on a serving dish, and sprinkle them with light soya sauce and sesame oil.

Soups

The quality of Chinese soups is based entirely on the quality of the stock used, and the same is true of Chinese vegetarian soups. Once the vegetarian stock is available (page 30), the eventual character and quality of the soup is determined by adding briefly cooked ingredients to simmer for a short while in the stock. These ingredients may vary from leaf vegetables to vegetables such as tomato, cucumber or watercress which do not need much cooking; to pickles of all types; and rehydrated dried vegetables, some of which are best added after a short period of stir-frying in a limited amount of oil. This process, we Chinese believe, allows the flavour of the ingredients to be 'exploded' by the heat into the oil and thereby more effectively communicated into the body of the soup.

Tofu soups have tofu or bean curd added as one of the more substantial ingredients incorporated in the chain of ingredients – usually as one of the last ingredients added, since tofu hardly needs much heating or cooking at all. Tofu is not added to contribute to the flavour of the soup, but more often as a contrast to the flavour and texture of the main body of the soup and, as such, it often has the effect of giving added character as well as substance to the soup.

Tofu soups are often simply a follow-on from the making of ordinary vegetarian soups, so I shall be including only a few recipes for them. Soya milk and soya mash can also be added to enrich soups: soya mash is usually added at an early stage and left to boil and simmer at length with the beans, cereals and root vegetables in the preparation of the original stock, while soya milk is added in the latter stages of preparation mainly to vary the flavour and increase the nutritiousness of the soup.

Chinese Vegetarian Stock

Basic Chinese vegetarian broth is prepared by boiling and simmering together, for example, 900 g (2 lb) mixed cereals: soya beans, sweet corn (cut into sections), soya mash, lentils, peanuts, broad beans (or any three of these items) in 3.5–4 litres (6–7 pints) of water for 1½ hours, followed by adding any three of the following items: potato, carrot, turnip, parsnip, broccoli stem, cauliflower stem, asparagus stem, mushroom stem. Boil and simmer together for a further 1½ hours. After 3 hours of boiling and slow simmering, the contents of the pan should be strained through muslin or cloth placed in a sieve or colander. If the resulting broth is too strong or too thick, water may be added to dilute. Since in these modern days many excellent vegetarian stock cubes are readily available (or such items as yeast extract, Vesop, Vecon vegetable stock), a small amount of these may be added to strengthen or improve the flavour of the stock.

Once the broth or stock is obtained, the preparation of a vast variety of Chinese vegetarian soups becomes a quick and simple matter. At this stage dark-coloured ingredients, such as soya sauce or Marmite, should only be added for seasoning if the soup is meant to be dark. This is often the case with tofu soups, since tofu is creamy white in colour and bland and subtle in flavour. It is therefore well set off when contrasted with a dark and highly savoury soup.

Hot and Sour Soup
This is a popular and classic Chinese soup. It is very satisfying, and especially good in winter, being hot, strong and substantial.
Serves 4–5, with rice and other dishes

50–75 g (2–3 oz) bamboo shoots	2 tbs vegetable oil
2 slices root-ginger	1 tbs chopped spring onion
1 medium-sized onion	1 tbs chopped coriander leaves
1 egg	2 tsp sesame oil
2 vegetarian stock cubes	*Hot and Sour Sauce*:
1.2 litres (2 pints) vegetarian stock	2 tbs light soya sauce
	3 tbs wine vinegar
2 tbs dark soya sauce	½ tsp freshly ground black pepper
2 cakes bean curd	
6 medium-sized Chinese dried mushrooms	2 tbs cornflour blended in 5 tbs water

Cut bamboo shoots into matchstick shreds. Cut root-ginger into thin, half-matchstick shreds. Cut onion into thin slices. Beat egg lightly in a bowl or cup. Dissolve stock cubes in the stock, and add soya sauce. Cut bean curd into sugar-lump-sized cubes. Soak mushrooms in boiling water for half an hour, remove stems and cut caps into shreds.

Heat vegetable oil in a saucepan. When hot, add ginger, onion and mushrooms and stir over medium heat for 1½ minutes. Add bamboo shoots and stir them in for 2 minutes. Pour in the stock. When the contents boil, allow them to simmer together for 5 minutes. Stir the hot and sour mixture until the ingredients are well blended, and stir this into the soup, which should then thicken. When the soup starts to bubble again, beat the egg again and pour it in a thin stream along the prongs of a fork into the soup, trailing the stream evenly over the whole surface of the soup. The egg should set immediately, forming what we call in China an 'egg-flower' effect in the soup. Now add the bean curd, which will increase the volume of the soup. Allow the soup to cook gently over medium heat for 3 more minutes.

The soup can be served by transferring it into a large common soup bowl or tureen (for people to help themselves from), or it can be divided into 4–5 individual soup bowls, and sprinkled with a pinch of chopped spring onion and coriander, and sesame oil.

Mashed Bean Curd Soup with Sweet Corn and Mushrooms
This is another substantial and satisfying soup. Good to serve to add substance to a meal.
Serves 4–5, with rice and other dishes

6 medium-sized Chinese dried mushrooms
6 medium-sized firm button mushrooms
25 g (1 oz) Sichuan hot Ja Tsai pickle
1½ cakes bean curd
2 tbs vegetable oil
2 spring onions (cut into 5-mm/ ¼-inch shavings)

100 g (4 oz) sweet corn
1.2 litres (2 pints) vegetarian stock
1 vegetarian stock cube
1 tbs light soya sauce
3–4 tbs green peas
1½ tbs cornflour blended in 4 tbs water
2 tsp sesame oil

Soak dried mushrooms in boiling water for half an hour. Remove stems, and roughly chop caps, retaining the mushroom water. Cut each button mushroom vertically into quarters. Coarsely chop pickle. Cut bean curd into sugar-lump-sized cubes.

Heat oil in a large saucepan. When hot, add both the dried and fresh mushrooms, pickle and spring onion. Stir them over medium heat for 3 minutes. Pour in the mushroom water. When the contents boil, leave them to simmer over low heat for 3 minutes. Add sweet corn and bean curd. Pour in the stock, in which the stock cube has been dissolved. Turn the heat up and bring contents to boil. Reduce heat and leave contents to simmer for 5 minutes. Add soya sauce and green peas. Stir them evenly into the soup. Stir the well-blended cornflour mixture into the soup. Stir the soup and sprinkle in the sesame oil. Serve in the same manner as the previous soup.

Egg-flower and Spring Onion Soup with Bean Curd

Egg-flower soup has always been regarded as one of the simplest of Chinese soups. Because of the speed and simplicity with which it can be made, it is frequently seen on the family dining table. Since the soup is meant to be consumed with rice throughout most of the meal, rather than to be eaten on its own, it should be served in a large soup bowl or tureen on the table so that diners can help themselves during the course of the meal.

Serves 4, with rice and other dishes

1 cake bean curd	1½ tbs light soya sauce
1 egg	1½ tbs coarsely chopped spring
1 vegetarian stock cube	onion
1.2 litres (2 pints) vegeterian stock	1½ tbs wine vinegar
	salt and pepper to taste

Cut bean curd into double matchstick shreds. Beat egg lightly. Dissolve stock cube in the stock. Heat stock in a saucepan. When it boils, reduce heat to a simmer. Drip the beaten egg into the soup along the prongs of a fork in a very thin stream, trailing the stream evenly over the surface of the soup. Add the bean curd shreds. When contents reboil, sprinkle them with soya sauce, chopped spring onion, vinegar, and adjust for seasoning with salt and pepper.

Turnip and Tomato Soup with Bean Curd

This is a clear soup, containing a substantial quantity of vegetables, which can be regarded partly as a soup and partly as a savoury dish to accompany rice.

Serves 4–5, with rice and other dishes

250 g (12 oz) turnip	1 vegetarian stock cube
1 cake bean curd	1 tbs light soya sauce
4–5 medium-sized tomatoes	1.2 litres (2 pints) vegetarian
900 ml (1½ pints) water	stock

Clean and cut turnip into 2.5-cm (1-inch) wedged pieces. Cut bean curd into cubes roughly the same size, and each tomato into quarters or sixths.

Heat turnip in water. Add stock cube and soya sauce, reduce heat to a simmer, and cook gently for half an hour. Add the stock. When contents reboil, add the bean curd and tomato. Simmer them together for 5 more minutes, and serve as in the previous recipe.

Bean Curd Soup with Seaweed, Peanuts, Mushrooms and Stem and Heart of Cabbage

As this should be an entirely clear soup, only water will be used in the cooking rather than vegetarian stock, since the latter is often cloudy, and it is a laborious process to remove all the cloudiness. This is a black and white soup: the mushroom, seaweed and fungi being all black and the bean curd being entirely white. The stem of the cabbage, tenderized by the cooking, provides some large pieces of distinctly vegetable-tasting ingredients to bite into. This is a rich but clear soup which can be served in individual bowls, or in a large common soup bowl or tureen for the diners to help themselves from during the course of the meal.

Serves 4–5, with rice and other dishes

40 g (1½ oz) hair seaweed
15–20 g (½–¾ oz) Chinese 'tree-ear' fungi
6–8 medium-sized Chinese dried mushrooms
3 slices root-ginger
25 g (1 oz) Sichuan hot pickle
2 small young Chinese *bak choi* or savoy cabbage
2½ tbs vegetable oil
2 cakes bean curd
50 g (2 oz) roasted peanuts
1.5 litres (2½ pints) water
1 vegetarian stock cube
1½ tbs light soya sauce
salt and pepper to taste

Soak seaweed and fungi in hot water for 10 minutes, and strain. Soak dried mushrooms in 300 ml (½ pint) boiling water for half an hour, retaining the water. Remove stems, and cut caps into quarters. Cut ginger and pickle into fine shreds. Remove all the outer leaves of the cabbage (for other uses), and the root ends of the stems. Cut the heart and stem of the cabbage into 4–5-cm (1½–2-inch) pieces. Cut bean curd into 2.5-cm (1-inch) cubes.

Heat oil in a large saucepan. When hot, add mushrooms and peanuts and stir in the hot oil for 2 minutes. Add ginger and pickle and continue to stir for 2 or more minutes. Pour in the mushroom water, and add the cabbage stem. When contents start to boil, reduce heat and leave to simmer for 5 minutes. Add the heart of the cabbage, fungi and seaweed and pour in the water. Bring contents to boil, reduce heat and leave the contents to simmer over gentle heat for half an hour. Add bean curd, stock cube and soya sauce, and adjust for seasoning with salt and pepper.

Soya Beans, Bean Sprouts and Bean Curd Soup

As this is a substantial soup it can be consumed throughout the meal as an additional dish.
Serves 5–6, with rice and other dishes

225 g (8 oz) dried soya beans
450 g (1 lb) fresh bean sprouts
2 cakes bean curd
3½–4 tbs vegetable oil
1.2 litres (2 pints) water
600 ml (1 pint) vegetarian stock
1 vegetarian stock cube
1 tsp salt
1 tsp sugar
1 tbs light soya sauce
1 tsp sesame oil

Soak soya beans in water overnight, or for at least 24 hours. Drain well. Clean and shake bean sprouts in clean water to discard their roots, or as many of them as possible. Set them aside. Cut bean curd into large sugar-lump-sized cubes.

Heat oil in a saucepan. When hot, add the beans, and stir-fry over medium heat for 4–5 minutes. Add the sprouts, and continue to turn and stir-fry for 3–4 minutes. Add the water, and bring contents to boil. Reduce heat to a simmer, and cook gently for a further hour.

Add the bean curd, stock and crumbled stock cube, salt, sugar and soya sauce. When the contents start to boil, simmer gently for 2 minutes. Sprinkle the soup with sesame oil.

Spinach and Bean Curd Soup
Serves 4–5, with rice and other dishes

225 kg (8 oz) fresh spinach	1 vegetarian stock cube
2 cloves garlic	1 tbs soya sauce
3½ tbs vegetable oil	1 cake bean curd
1 tsp salt	1½ tbs cornflour blended in
600 ml (1 pint) water	4 tbs water
600 ml (1 pint) vegetarian stock	1 tsp sesame oil

Wash spinach and drain well. Pile it up and slice it at 2.5-cm (1-inch) intervals. Coarsely crush the garlic.

Heat oil in a large deep wok. When hot, add the spinach and salt and turn in the oil until the vegetable has softened and given out its water. Drain the water away with the aid of a perforated spoon. Add water and bring contents to boil; add the vegetarian stock, stock cube and soya sauce. When contents reboil, add the bean curd pieces. Cook gently for a further 4–5 minutes, turning the contents over gently a few times so as to mix the ingredients more evenly. Sprinkle in the blended cornflour and sesame oil. Give the contents one more turn and serve in the same manner as in the previous recipe.

Bean Curd Soup with Fava Beans and Chinese Snow Pickle
Like most bean curd soups this is a substantial soup. It can be served either as a soup or as a main course dish, along with other dishes served during the course of the meal.
Serves 4–5, with rice and other dishes

225 g (8 oz) fava beans	600 ml (1 pint) vegetarian stock
1–2 red chillies	1 vegetarian stock cube
50–75 g (2–3 oz) snow pickle	2 tbs light soya sauce
1½ cakes bean curd	1 tsp sugar
2 tbs vegetable oil	pepper to taste
600 ml (1 pint) water	1 tbs sesame oil

Soak beans overnight (or slightly longer) until the seed coats can be easily removed. Rinse the beans under running water. Place them in a saucepan. Add fresh water, and boil them for 30 minutes.

Drain and mash them into a purée. Top and tail the chillies, and remove the pips. Chop them and the snow pickle into a coarse mince. Cut bean curd into sugar-lump-sized pieces.

Heat oil in a saucepan. When hot, add the pickle and chillies and stir-fry them together for 2 minutes. Add the water and and bring contents to boil. Add the bean purée and the vegetarian stock and stock cube. When contents reboil, reduce heat to low, add bean curd and allow contents to simmer gently for a further 5–6 minutes, stirring gently all the time. Add soya sauce, sugar and pepper to taste. Sprinkle with sesame oil and serve.

Stir-fried Bean Curd Dishes

There are two types of bean curd dishes. Either they contain 'pressed bean curd', which is cut into strips or thin slices and stir-fried with a variety of vegetables, similarly cut into strips or sliced; or 'mashed bean curd', which is stir-fried with strong or flavoursome ingredients and sauces. This latter type is usually served as a topping on plain boiled rice or noodles, while the former is usually served as an individual dish, along with other dishes on the table, and accompanied by rice or other bulk foods, such as noodles, steamed buns, soft rice (or rice-porridge) or vegetable fried rice.

Pressed Bean Curd

Pressed bean curd is made by extracting more water out of the bean curd. This can be done when the bean curd is still being made, at the stage when the freshly formed curd is wrapped and covered with muslin or cloth, and a weight is placed on top of it to press it into shape (page 21). Now, if the weight placed on top of the curd is increased by three or four times (to 3.5–4 kg/8–10 lb), and the time during which the curd is being pressed is lengthened to over eight hours or overnight, the water in the curd should have drained out slowly and much more thoroughly. The resultant substance should be much drier and firmer in texture than usual. In China this firmer and drier form of bean curd is simply called the dried bean curd or *toufukan*.

Processing the dried bean curd is not complete until it has been submerged in a marinade consisting of 4–5 tbs of soya sauce added to 600 ml (1 pint) of water together with 1 tbs sugar, 2 tsp salt, and 3–4 pieces of star-anise. The mixture is brought very slowly and gently to the boil, and the dried bean curd allowed to simmer in the marinade for a further 7–8 minutes. It should then be removed from heat, and the dried bean curd submerged in the marinade overnight, after which it should be drained, and cut into strips, slices or cubes (or into any shape or size which is best suited to the culinary purpose for which it is intended).

Dried bean curd can also be produced from ready-made bean curd or tofu simply by laying the bean curd pieces out in a single layer, wrapping them with muslin or cheesecloth and subjecting them to 2.75–3.5 kg (6–8 lb) of pressure overnight applied by a flat weight on the bean curd. The much firmer and drier form of bean curd is then slowly and shortly cooked in the same marinade as described above, and then left submerged in it overnight. When the dried bean curd is drained, it is ready to be cut into sizes appropriate for whatever culinary purpose.

Stir-fry of Shredded Pressed Bean Curd with Three Shredded Ingredients

This is a dish which is popular in the Lower Yangtze areas. It is served on the table, along with other dishes, for consuming with rice.
Serves 4–5, with rice and other dishes

100–150 g (4–5 oz) *toufukan* or
  pressed bean curd
2–3 young carrots
50–75 g (2–3 oz) mangetouts or
  snow peas
4–5 slices root-ginger
3 tbs vegetable oil
4 tbs vegetarian stock

Sauce:
1½ tbs soya sauce
½ tbs yellow bean sauce (paste)
1 tbs hoisin sauce
1½ tbs dry sherry
1 tsp sugar
1 tbs sesame oil

Cut pressed bean curd into 1½ matchstick-sized strips. Scrape clean and cut carrots and mangetouts into similar-sized strips. Cut ginger into finer shreds.

Heat vegetable oil in a frying pan or wok. When hot, add ginger and stir in the hot oil for half a minute, followed by the carrots and mangetouts, and stir and turn them, over medium heat, for 2 minutes. Finally, add the pressed bean curd strips and the vegetarian stock. Continue to stir and turn them together for 3 more minutes, or until nearly all the liquid has evaporated.

Now add all the sauce ingredients and mix them together with all the shredded vegetables in the pan. Continue to stir and turn for about 2–2½ minutes, or until the pressed bean curd and the vegetables are evenly coated by the sauce.

Hot-tossed Pressed Bean Curd with Celery and Sichuan Ja Tsai Pickle

This is quite a spicy dish, and is suitable to serve and eat with quantities of plain boiled rice.
Serves 4–5, with rice and other dishes

100g (4 oz) *toufukan* or pressed
  bean curd
100–175g (4–6 oz) celery
40–50g (1½–2 oz) Sichuan hot
  pickle
3 slices root-ginger
2 spring onions

3½–4 tbs vegetable oil
Sauce or Dressing:
1½ tbs soya sauce
½ tsp sugar
5 tbs vegetarian stock
½ vegetarian stock cube
2 tsp chilli sauce

Cut pressed bean curd and celery into double matchstick strips, and pickle and ginger into fine shreds, and spring onions into 5-cm (2-inch) sections.

Heat oil in a frying pan or wok. When hot, add first the ginger and pickle. Stir them in the hot oil for half a minute. Add the celery, pressed bean curd and spring onion. Continue to stir and turn over medium heat for 2½ minutes. Add all the sauce ingredients and continue to stir and turn over high heat for another 2 minutes.

Hot-tossed Pressed Bean Curd with Shredded Fresh Bean Curd, Mushrooms and Celery

This is a highly savoury dish. Two fresh ingredients – bean curd and mushrooms – and two seasoned ingredients – marinated, pressed bean curd and dried mushrooms – are tossed and stir-fried together in flavoured oil, with shredded celery providing a contrast in texture. Serve with other dishes and quantities of plain boiled rice.
Serves 5–6, with rice and other dishes

1 cake bean curd
75g (3 oz) dried, seasoned,
  pressed bean curd
6 medium-sized Chinese dried
  mushrooms
225g (8 oz) large button
  mushrooms
2 spring onions
3 slices root-ginger
2 cloves garlic
4 tbs vegetable oil

¾ tsp salt
1 stick celery
5 tbs vegetarian stock
Sauce:
1½ tbs light soya sauce
1 tsb hoisin sauce
2 tsp chilli sauce
1½ tbs dry sherry
1 tsp sugar
1 tbs tomato purée

Cut both bean curds into double matchstick strips. Soak dried mushrooms for half an hour in boiling water. Discard stems and cut the caps and the fresh mushrooms into strips similar to the bean curd. Cut spring onion into 5-mm (¼-inch) shavings (separate the white from the greens). Shred ginger, coarsely crush and mince garlic.

Heat oil in a frying pan or wok. When hot, add ginger, garlic, whites of spring onion, dried mushrooms and pressed bean curd. Stir-fry them together for 3 minutes over medium heat. Add fresh mushrooms, salt, celery and stock, and continue to stir-fry for 3 more minutes. Add fresh bean curd, and all the sauce ingredients. Turn and stir all the ingredients together for 1½ minutes, until they are all evenly mixed and well coated.

Deep-fried Bean Curd Stir-fried with Mushrooms and Broccoli

This is another rice-accompanying dish often seen on Chinese tables. The bean curd provides the meat-like protein, the mushrooms its savouriness, and the lightly cooked broccoli the crisp taste of fresh vegetables.

Serves 4–5, with rice and other dishes

1½ cakes bean curd	4 tbs vegetarian stock
vegetable oil for deep-frying	*Sauce*:
6–8 medium-sized Chinese	2 tbs light soya sauce
dried mushrooms	1 tbs hoisin sauce
1 medium-sized onion	2 tsp chilli sauce
225 g (8 oz) broccoli	1½ tbs dry sherry
3 tbs vegetable oil	1 tsp sugar
3 slices root-ginger	

Cut bean curd into 2.5 × 4-cm (1 × 1½-inch) flat pieces. Deep-fry them in hot oil for 2–2½ minutes until the surfaces are somewhat firm and yellow in colour. Drain thoroughly. Soak mushrooms in boiling water for half an hour. Discard stems and cut caps into halves. Cut onion into thin slices. Break broccoli into individual florets and cut stem into 2.5-cm (1-inch) wedged pieces.

Heat vegetable oil in a large frying pan or wok. When hot, add onion, ginger, broccoli stems and mushrooms and stir-fry in the hot oil for 2 minutes, to season the oil. Add broccoli and stock and continue to stir-fry for 1½ minutes and cook under cover for 1½ minutes. Pour the sauce ingredients over the contents and continue to turn and stir-fry all ingredients together for a further 1½ minutes.

Vegetarian Mu Shou Rou or Shredded Bean Curd with 'Golden Needles' (Tiger Lily Buds), Mushrooms, 'Wood Ears' (Tree Fungi) and Eggs

This is a favourite dish of north China. Its vegetarian version is popular throughout the country.
Serves 4–5, with rice and other dishes

1 cake bean curd	3 tbs vegetable oil
vegetable oil for deep-frying	½ tsp salt
50 g (2 oz) 'wood ears' (available at Chinese foodstores)	3 eggs
	1 tsp sesame oil
50 g (2 oz) 'golden needles' (available at Chinese foodstores)	*Sauce*:
	1½ tbs light soya sauce
4–5 medium-sized Chinese dried mushrooms	1 tbs yellow bean sauce (paste)
	1 tbs dry sherry
2 spring onions	1 tsp sugar
2 cloves garlic	2 tbs vegetarian stock

Cut bean curd into double matchstick shreds. Deep-fry for 1½ minutes, and drain thoroughly. Soak 'wood ears' and 'golden needles' in water for 4–5 minutes, rinse and drain. Soak mushrooms in boiling water for half an hour, and drain. Remove and discard the stems. Cut each cap into quarters. Cut spring onions into 5-mm (¼-inch) shavings (separating the white from the greens). Crush and chop garlic.

Heat half the vegetable oil in a frying pan or wok. When hot, add the whites of the spring onion, mushrooms and garlic. Stir-fry them together for 1½ minutes. Add salt, bean curd, 'wood ears' and 'golden needles'. Stir-fry them together for 1½ minutes over medium heat and then put aside.

Heat the remaining oil in another pan or wok. Beat the eggs lightly and pour them in. When about to set, add half the spring onions, stir and break egg up into 2.5–4-cm (1–1½-inch) pieces, and withdraw from heat.

In the meanwhile, place the original pan or wok over medium heat. When the ingredients start to sizzle, pour in all the sauce ingredients, and turn and stir them around quickly, until all the ingredients are well coated. Add the eggs into the same pan or wok and turn and toss them together with the other ingredients. Sprinkle them with the remainder of the spring onion and the sesame oil, and serve.

Stir-fried Bean Curd with French Beans in Hot Sauce

This is a spicy dish, suitable for consuming with quantities of plain boiled rice.
Serves 4–5, with rice and other dishes

350 g (12 oz) French beans	1 tbs hoisin sauce
1½ cakes bean curd	½ tbs yellow bean sauce (paste)
3 cloves garlic	2 tsp chilli sauce
3½ tbs vegetable oil	2 tsp red oil (Chinese chilli oil –
½ tsp salt	optional)
Sauce:	1 tbs tomato purée
1 tbs light soya sauce	

Top and tail the French beans, and cut each piece into two. Boil them in ample water for 2 minutes, and drain well. Cut bean curd into 2-cm (¾-inch) cubes. Crush and chop garlic.

Heat oil in a frying pan or wok. When hot, add garlic, salt and French beans. Stir-fry them over medium heat for 2½ minutes. Add the bean curd pieces, and turn them lightly with the beans for 1½ minutes. Pour in all the sauce ingredients. Turn and stir them together for 1 minute. Cook and turn for 1½ more minutes, and serve.

Hot-tossed Diced Pressed Bean Curd with Green Peas, Bamboo Shoots, Dried Mushrooms, Straw Mushrooms and Courgette or Aubergine Cubes

Another somewhat spicy dish, excellent with plain boiled rice.
Serves 5–6, with other dishes

225 g (8 oz) pressed bean curd
75–100 g (3–4 oz) bamboo shoots
1 medium-sized courgette or
  1 small aubergine
4–5 medium-sized Chinese
  dried mushrooms
1 medium-sized onion
2 cloves garlic
1 green and 1 red chilli

3 tbs vegetable oil
½ tsp salt
1 tbs Chinese winter pickle
  (Dung Tsai)
1 small can straw mushrooms
75 g (3 oz) green peas (fresh or
  frozen)
2 tsp sesame oil

Sauce:
1½ tbs light soya sauce
2 tsp red bean curd 'cheese'
1½ tbs dry sherry

6 tbs vegetarian stock
1 tsp sugar
1½ tsp chilli sauce

Cut pressed bean curd into cubes the size of half a sugar lump. Cut bamboo shoots and courgette or aubergine into similar-sized cubes (leaving on the skin). Soak dried mushrooms in boiling water for half an hour, discard stems, and cut caps into quarters. Cut onion into very thin slices, crush and chop garlic, shred chillies (discarding pips).

Heat oil in a frying pan or wok. When hot, add onion, garlic and chilli and stir-fry them together for half a minute over medium heat. Add salt, pressed bean curd, dried mushrooms and pickle, and stir-fry them all together over high heat for 1½ minutes. Add bamboo shoots, straw mushrooms, peas, courgette or aubergine, and continue to stir-fry for a further 1½ minutes. Add the sauce ingredients, turn and stir the contents of the wok or frying pan vigorously. Place a lid over the pan, reduce heat to medium-low. Leave to cook gently for 5 minutes. Remove lid and sprinkle contents with sesame oil, and serve.

Steamed Stuffed Cucumber Cups with Mashed Bean Curd and Chopped
Pressed Bean Curd

These cucumber cups, covered with a reddish-brown sauce, make a picturesque dish and a useful starter for a Chinese vegetarian meal. Serves 4–6, with other dishes

2 large cucumbers
50 g (2 oz) pressed bean curd
1 cake bean curd
4 medium-sized dried
  mushrooms
1 clove garlic
2 slices root-ginger
2 spring onions
3 tbs vegetable oil
½ tsp salt

Sauce:
1½ tbs light soya sauce
1½ tsp red bean curd 'cheese'
1 tbs hoisin sauce
½ tbs Sichuan Tou-Pan soya
  paste sauce
2 tbs vegetarian stock
1 tbs red oil chilli sauce
1 tbs vegetable oil

Clean and cut cucumber into regular 6-cm (2½-inch) sections. Scoop out the insides to a depth of 5 cm (2 inches), making cucumber cups with 1 cm (½ inch) left at the bottom of each cup. Chop pressed bean curd into coarse grains, and mash the bean curd. Soak the dried mushrooms in boiling water for half an hour. Discard stems and coarsely chop caps. Finely chop garlic and ginger. Cut spring onion into shavings (keeping the white separate from the greens).

Heat oil in a frying pan or wok. When hot, add the ginger, garlic, whites of spring onion, salt, and chopped pressed bean curd, and stir-fry together over medium heat for 2 minutes. Add the mashed bean curd, and continue to stir-fry all the ingredients together for a further 2 minutes.

Stuff the stir-fried ingredients into the cucumber cups until each cup is filled up to the brim. Arrange the cups, well spaced out, on a flat heatproof dish. Insert the dish into a steamer and steam vigorously for 5–6 minutes.

While the cucumber cups are steaming, heat and stir the sauce ingredients together in a small saucepan, until they are well blended and beginning to boil.

Remove the dish from the steamer, and drain away any water which may have collected during the steaming. Pour the sauce from the small saucepan over the contents of the cucumber cups, and serve.

Bean Curd Skin 'Sticks'

These are made from the skin of bean curd milk, and are

usually available in stick form, 15–23 cm (6–9 inches) long. They are dry, firm and crispy in texture, and require softening by soaking in hot water, or cooking in stock. In Chinese cooking they are mostly used in braised 'semi-soup' dishes, which occur frequently on the Chinese table as a variation from stir-fried dishes. They are also sometimes included in stir-fried dishes, mostly in the context of hard vegetables, where the ingredients need to be cooked or braised for a somewhat longer time than is normally required in stir-frying.

Braised Bean Curd Skin Sticks with Transparent Noodles (or Bean-starch Threads)

This is a useful semi-soup dish for serving at an informal meal as an alternative to quick-fried dishes.
Serves 5–6, with other dishes

3 bean curd skin sticks	3 tbs vegetable oil
25 g (1 oz) 'golden needles'	2 slices root-ginger, shredded
75–100 g (3–4 oz) transparent noodles	½ tsp salt
	450 ml (¾ pint) vegetarian stock
100–150 g (4–5 oz) broccoli	75–100 g (3–4 oz) bean sprouts
3 medium-sized slices Sichuan Ja Tsai pickle	2 tbs light soya sauce

Break bean curd milk sticks into quarters. Add to a large saucepan of warm water. Bring to the boil slowly. Turn off heat, leave to soak for a further 30–40 minutes, and drain. Soak 'golden needles' in hot water for 5 minutes and drain. Also soak transparent noodles for 5 minutes, and drain. Cut both into 4-cm (1½-inch) sections, and the bean curd sticks into similar-sized sections. Break off the broccoli florets and cut them into 4-cm (1½-inch) pieces. Shred the pickle.

Heat oil in a frying pan. When hot, add ginger and pickle followed by salt, bean curd skins and broccoli. Stir them together with the other ingredients for 2½ minutes. Pour in the stock. When it boils, add the bean sprouts and noodles. Allow the contents to simmer for 8 minutes, then add soya sauce.

Sautéed Bean Curd Sticks in Mushroom Oil with Asparagus and Fresh Mushrooms

This is a very tasty combination of foods which can be served with the majority of other dishes and consumed with rice. The enjoyment of the chewiness of the bean curd skin together with crunchy or soft vegetables is a cultivated taste which we Chinese appreciate a lot.
Serves 5–6, with other dishes

4–5 sticks bean curd skin
450 g (1 lb) fresh asparagus
225 g (8 oz) fresh button mushrooms
2 tbs vegetable oil
½ tsp salt
5–6 tbs vegetarian stock
1½ tbs light soya sauce
2 tsp soya 'cheese' (white or red)

4–5 tbs mushroom oil with sautéed mushrooms (see below)
Mushroom oil:
6–8 medium-sized dried mushrooms
450 g (1 lb) fresh mushrooms
6 tbs vegetable oil
1½ tbs light soya sauce

Prepare the mushroom oil. Soak dried mushrooms in boiling water for 30 minutes, and drain. Discard stems and cut caps into shreds. Clean and cut fresh mushrooms vertically through stems into quarters or sixths.

Heat oil in a saucepan or wok. When hot, add the dried mushrooms, and stir-fry for 1½ minutes. Add the fresh mushrooms, and stir-fry them together for 3 minutes over medium heat. Add soya sauce, reduce heat to low and continue to stir-fry for 2 minutes. Leave contents to simmer gently and sauté for a further 8 minutes, stirring and turning occasionally. When all the moisture has evaporated, the mushroom substance and oil should be very flavoursome. They can be used independently by straining the oil from the mushrooms, or simply by using spoonfuls of the oil and the fried mushrooms together.

Break each stick of bean curd milk into quarters. Add to a large pan of water, and bring slowly to boil. Leave to soak for 30 minutes, and drain. Cut them into 4-cm (1½-inch) regular sections. Clean and cut asparagus in 6–7.5-cm (2½–3-inch) sections, discarding the roots and dividing the tips from the harder, whiter sections of the stems. Clean the button mushrooms and cut them vertically into quarters.

Heat oil in a saucepan or wok. When hot, add the white sections of asparagus, bean curd milk sticks and salt, and stir-fry them together for 2 minutes. Add vegetarian stock and sauté the contents over low heat for 4–5 minutes. Now add the asparagus tips, fresh mushrooms, soya sauce, soya 'cheese', mushroom oil and sautéed mushrooms. Stir and mix all the ingredients together for 2½ minutes over medium heat. Reduce heat to low and allow contents to simmer-sauté together for 2½ minutes.

Sautéed Bean Curd Sticks in Mushroom Oil with Baby Corn and Broccoli

Since mushroom oil and sautéed mushrooms (see above) are such flavoursome ingredients they can naturally be used to cook with other combinations of ingredients, in this case with baby corn and broccoli. This dish provides a colourful mixture of vegetables and goes well with Chinese pasta or plain boiled rice.
Serves 5–6, with other dishes

350g (12 oz) broccoli
175–225g (6–8 oz) baby corn
3–4 sticks bean curd skin
3 tbs vegetable oil
1½ tbs light soya sauce

4 tbs vegetarian stock
5–6 tbs mushroom oil with
  sautéed mushrooms
2 tsp sesame oil

Break broccoli into individual florets. Cut stems into 4-cm (1½-inch) wedged slices. Drain the baby corn. Prepare the bean curd skin as in the previous recipe.

Heat oil in a frying pan or wok. When hot, add the wedged pieces of broccoli stems and bean curd skin and stir-fry them over medium heat for 2 minutes. Add soya sauce, stock, baby corn and broccoli florets. Turn and stir them together for 1 minute and leave them to sauté together for 2½ minutes, or until most of the moisture has evaporated. Add the mushroom oil and sautéed mushrooms and stir with the other ingredients for 1 minute. Leave all the ingredients to sauté together over low heat for 3 minutes. Sprinkle with sesame oil. Stir, turn once more and serve.

2 Eggs

Eggs usually come in four main forms or styles: marbled tea eggs, soya eggs, salt eggs, and 'hundred-year-old eggs'.

Marbled tea eggs are hardboiled eggs which have had their shells slightly cracked, are reboiled in strong tea, and left to soak in the latter for a period of time. The process not only allows the tea flavour to penetrate, but also enables the small amount of tea which seeps through the cracked shells to form a marbled pattern on the white surface of the boiled eggs.

Soya eggs are hardboiled eggs, with their shells removed, which are cooked for a short while in soya sauce. This cooking and soaking rapidly causes the eggs to turn dark brown: the colour of the soya sauce. The soya sauce coating not only helps the eggs to keep for longer, but its rich salty flavour and the contrast with the egg white underneath also seems to make them more appealing to eat with rice, especially with rice-porridge or *congee*, which is standard food for a Chinese breakfast. Soya eggs are one of the most frequently seen items on the Chinese breakfast table, and often eaten while travelling and at picnics.

Salt eggs are usually produced using duck or goose eggs which are boiled and steeped in brine. This process causes the yolk to turn orangey red in colour. Because of the saltiness of such eggs, they are also a favourite item on the Chinese breakfast table, where bland rice-porridge (*congee*) is consumed and the majority of accompaniments served have to be pickled or salty to provide a contrast.

Hundred-year-old eggs is of course a nickname. It would probably be more accurate to call them 'pickled eggs' since they are lengthily 'pickled' in a mixture of mud and lime. When bought – they are hardly ever made at home, as with the other types of eggs – they are not only encrusted in thick mud but a layer of chopped straw is also embedded. This helps to keep the eggs apart while they are stored together in a large earthen jar to mature for several months. During this period, the eggs have to be turned around a number of times. The eggs (usually duck eggs) are in fact very slowly 'cooked' by the heat generated when water is added to the mud-and-lime mixture. After the necessary period of 'incubating', the egg white will have turned dark green in colour, and the yolk orangey green. Between them they emit a sulphurous odour which presages an eggy savouriness that is highly appealing to the cultivated and converted. Apart from being eaten for breakfast, these eggs are also often cut up into wedges and served as hors d'oeuvres at a multicourse party dinner; alternatively they are steamed together in a savoury egg custard along with tea eggs, salt eggs or quail eggs in a multi-egg dish, where the three or four different types and colours of egg are presented together, all partly immersed in the yellowness of the custard. Quail eggs are not considered serious food in China because of their small size, but they are useful for decorative purposes in an assembly of items for a large party dish.

As already indicated, these four types of eggs can be eaten on their own, or with one another; or they can be cut into slices, wedges or smaller pieces and further cooked by steaming or stir-frying with other food materials to create a large number of other dishes to which these 'seasoned' eggs can contribute their own inimitable flavour.

An ordinary beaten egg is of course even more versatile than seasoned eggs. Apart from being extremely quick and convenient to cook, it can easily be combined with most vegetables by stir-frying them together; or if the vegetables are easily tenderized, they can be steamed together in an egg custard. Because the method of steaming is prevalent in

Chinese kitchens and steamed savoury egg custard is emi-
nently suitable and appealing to eat with rice, it is an
extremely popular dish in Chinese home cooking.

But it is in stir-frying that eggs produce by far the largest
number of dishes, and they can in most cases be prepared and
produced in a very short time. Chinese stir-fried egg dishes
are something in between a Western scrambled egg and an
omelette – the beaten eggs cooking in a pan are usually stirred
just before they set. If other ingredients are incorporated and
cooked together with them, the result is usually like a Spanish
omelette. The difference lies in the fact that the Spanish use
potato in their omelettes; we Chinese would only incorporate
other ingredients and food materials either to improve or vary
the flavour or colour of the dish (we would hardly incorporate
potato which would only increase the bulk!). To achieve this
in our vegetarian cooking, we use a line of chopped pickles
first of all to season and flavour the oil used, and at the end the
egg dish is sprinkled with a small overlay of finely and freshly
chopped aromatic ingredients, such as chopped chives,
spring onions, coriander leaves or flower petals supported by
some wine and soya sauce. In between, larger quantities of
quick-to-cook colourful vegetables, such as tomato, red or
green peppers, spinach, bean sprouts, mushrooms, broccoli
florets, asparagus tips, and so on, may be incorporated. But, in
order to avoid spoiling any of the ingredients which must not,
at all costs, be allowed in Chinese cooking, some of these food
materials are stir-fried separately, and only thrown together
with the beaten egg in the last moment's final assembly when
the egg has still not quite set.

Hence, in such cooking, timing is of the essence, and great
dishes can be created out of ordinary materials. But to ease the
demand made on the skill of the cook, equally appealing
dishes can be produced by cooking the bulky and colourful
vegetables quite independently of the 'scrambled omelette'.
These can be arranged in a bed on a serving dish with the egg
placed on top. Just a word on the effect of wine and soya sauce
on Chinese scrambled omelettes: a small amount of hot wine

(Chinese rice wine is usually heated before drinking), and an even smaller amount of good quality soya sauce (1 to 2 tbs) poured over the omelette just before serving, are quite capable of lifting what amounts to an ordinary household dish to *haute cuisine* by any standards. But the combined use of chopped spring onion (called *chung hua*) and soya sauce is a must when serving stir-fried eggs, as they seem to have the effect of emphasizing the egginess as well as increasing the aromatic appeal.

Simple Stir-fried Eggs

Although there are many other dishes which can be eaten with rice, these stir-fried eggs have a unique appeal.
Serves 4–6, with other dishes

5–6 eggs	¼ tsp freshly ground pepper
4–5 tbs vegetable oil	1½ tbs good quality soya sauce
2½ tbs chopped spring onions or chives	

Beat eggs lightly with a fork, or a pair of chopsticks, for 10–15 seconds, or until blended.

Heat oil in a frying pan or wok. When hot, reduce heat to low. Pour in the beaten egg, and see that the latter spreads evenly over the pan. Sprinkle the egg evenly with half the spring onion and the pepper. Allow the egg to cook gently for about 1½–1¾ minutes, when it should be about three-quarters set. Turn and stir the eggs, and transfer them to a well-heated serving dish with a fish slice or perforated spoon (thus straining away any excess oil). When the eggs are still quite hot, sprinkle them with the remaining spring onion and soya sauce.

Stir-fried Eggs with Spinach

This is a simple but attractive dish, and extremely appealing with plain boiled rice.
Serves 6–8, with other dishes

350 g (12 oz) young spinach	1½ tsp sesame oil
3–4 cloves garlic	stir-fried egg mixture (see
4 tbs vegetable oil	above)
1 tsp salt	

Clean and wash the spinach and dry thoroughly. Remove the roots and tougher stems. Crush and coarsely chop garlic.

Heat oil in a frying pan or wok. When hot, add the garlic and stir-fry over medium heat for 15 seconds. Add salt and then the spinach, and spread evenly over the pan. After 30–45 seconds turn and stir-fry it over high heat for 1–1½ minutes. By this time the vegetable should be well glossed and lubricated by the hot oil.

Transfer the spinach on to a well-heated serving dish. Spread it out evenly over the dish, sprinkle with sesame oil, and place the stir-fried egg on top of the bed of spinach.

Stir-fried Egg with Soya-bean Mash, Peas and Straw Mushrooms
This is a fairly substantial dish, and should add bulk and nutrition to a family meal.
Serves 5–6, with other dishes

3–4 eggs	4–5 tbs straw mushrooms, or
1 tsp salt	firm button mushrooms
5 tbs vegetable oil	chopped to the same size as
2 cloves garlic, chopped	straw mushrooms
2 tbs snow pickle, coarsely	100–150 g (4–5 oz) soya-bean
chopped	mash (see page 37)
3–4 tbs green peas, fresh or	1½ tbs chopped spring onion
frozen	

Lightly beat eggs with ½ tsp salt for ten seconds. Heat 3 tbs oil in a frying pan or wok. When hot, add the garlic and pickle and stir-fry together for half a minute. Add peas, mushrooms and soya mash and stir-fry together over high heat for 2 minutes. Then push them to one side of the pan. Add remaining oil to the other side, and when this is hot, pour in the beaten egg. After 1 minute, and when the eggs have set, scramble them, and bring over the other ingredients in the pan to scramble together with the eggs. Reduce heat to low and sprinkle contents with chopped spring onion and remaining salt. Continue to stir-fry all the ingredients together for 1–1½ more minutes, and serve.

Stir-fried Eggs with Tomatoes
Serves 4–5, with other dishes

4–5 eggs	1¼ tsp salt
5 firm, medium-sized tomatoes	1½ tsp sugar
4½ tbs vegetable oil	1 tbs soya sauce
2 spring onions, chopped	1 tbs dry sherry
(separate white from greens)	pepper to taste
1–2 slices root-ginger, chopped	
into fine grains	

Beat eggs lightly with a fork or chopsticks for 10–15 seconds until blended. Cut each tomato into quarters.

Heat 2½ tbs vegetable oil in a frying pan or wok. When hot, add the whites of the spring onions and the ginger. Stir them in the hot oil for half a minute. Add the sliced tomatoes. Sprinkle them with salt and sugar. Turn and stir-fry them together for 1 minute, then push them to one side of the pan. Add the remaining oil to the other side. When hot, pour in the beaten eggs. After 1 minute, turn and stir-fry the eggs lightly for half a minute. Bring the tomatoes over to mix and stir-fry together with the eggs. Sprinkle them with soya sauce, spring onion greens, sherry and pepper. Turn and stir the contents together once more.

Transfer the contents on to a well-heated serving dish.

Stir-fried Eggs with Green Beans
This is another excellent dish to accompany rice.
Serves 4–5, with other dishes

225–350 g (8–12 oz) green beans	¾ tsp salt
2 cloves garlic	1 tsp sugar
4 eggs	1 tbs dry sherry
4½ tbs vegetable oil	1 tsp sesame oil

Boil the beans in water for 4–5 minutes (so that the skin can be more easily removed after cutting off both ends), drain and remove the skin. Crush and chop garlic. Beat the eggs lightly for 10–15 seconds until blended.

Heat 2½tbs oil in a frying pan or wok. When hot, add the beans and salt to stir-fry over medium heat for 1½ minutes. Add sugar and 4–5tbs water. Continue to stir-fry for a further 2 minutes, or until all the water has evaporated. Push the contents to one side of the pan. Pour the remainder of the oil into the other side of the pan. When hot, pour in the beaten eggs. After 1½ minutes, when the eggs have almost set, turn and stir-fry them for 15 seconds. Bring the beans over to turn, and stir with the eggs for half a minute. Sprinkle the contents with sherry and sesame oil. Turn and stir once more, and transfer the contents on to a well-heated serving dish.

Cauliflower Egg Fu-Yung

In China Fu-Yung is a term which applies to dishes cooked with only the whites of eggs. This is considered to be a more refined dish than the two previous recipes. Being completely white it is usually served along with darker dishes which have been cooked with soya sauce. Serves 4–5, with other dishes

1 medium-sized cauliflower	5tbs vegetable oil
1 small red sweet pepper	¾tbs Vesop (or other light
5 egg whites	vegetarian sauce)
3tsp cornflour	3–4tbs vegetarian stock
½tsp salt	1tbs dry sherry
3tbs top of the milk or cream	

Break cauliflower into individual florets (remove and discard most of the stem). Plunge them into boiling water to parboil for 2 minutes, and drain well. Cut pepper into thin strips, remove stem and discard pips.

Beat egg whites together with cornflour, salt and top of the milk (or cream) with fork or chopsticks or whisk vigorously for 2 minutes, until egg-milk is beginning to stiffen.

Heat 2½tbs oil in a frying pan or wok. When hot, add cauliflower, pepper, sauce and stock. Stir-fry them over high heat for 2 minutes. Reduce heat to medium-low and push them to one side of the pan. Add the remaining oil to the other side of the pan. When hot, add the egg-milk mixture. Stir and scramble for 1½ minutes, or until the egg white begins to set. Bring the vegetable over to mix, stir and turn with the egg. Sprinkle the contents with sherry, and serve.

Pearl River Boatmen's Multilayer Omelette
Although this dish is not considered as a particularly refined one, it is enjoyed by many because of its multiplicity of ingredients, and because of its being different from the ordinary stir-fried dishes.
Serves 6, with other dishes

1 tsp salt	75–100 g (3–4 oz) straw
6 eggs	mushrooms, or button
75–100 g (3–4 oz) bean sprouts	mushrooms chopped to half-
6 tbs vegetable oil	sugar-lump size
1 clove garlic, crushed and	2 spring onions cut into green
chopped	and white shavings
1½ tbs soya sauce	1½ tbs dry sherry

Add salt to eggs. Beat them together for 10–15 seconds until blended. Wash bean sprouts and dry thoroughly.

Heat 2½ tbs oil in a frying pan or wok. When hot, add garlic and bean sprouts. Stir-fry them over high heat for 1½ minutes, and spread them evenly over the pan. Pour one-third of the beaten eggs evenly over the pan. (Lift the handle of the pan so that the eggs will flow evenly over the pan.) As soon as the eggs set, lift the contents in one piece, with the aid of a fish slice, and transfer it on to a well-heated serving dish. Pour one-third of the soya sauce over the egg and bean sprouts.

Heat half the remaining oil in the pan. When hot, add the mushrooms and stir-fry them over high heat for 1 minute, and spread them evenly over the pan. Pour half the remaining beaten eggs over the mushrooms. (Lift the handle of the pan, so that the eggs will flow evenly over the surface.) As soon as the eggs set, lift the contents out in one piece, with the aid of a fish slice, and place squarely over the egg and bean sprouts which are already in the serving dish.

Pour the remaining oil into the pan. When hot, add the whites of the spring onion, stir them round a few times, and spread them evenly over the pan. Pour in the beaten egg, and see that it flows evenly over the pan. As soon as the egg sets, sprinkle with the greens of spring onion and the remaining soya sauce. Lift up the contents in one piece and place on top of the layers of egg and mushroom which are already in the serving dish.

Heat the sherry in the pan. As soon as it boils, pour it over the triple-layer omelette in the serving dish.

Fu-Yung Sauce

Chinese Fu-Yung sauce is a white sauce made principally with egg white beaten together with stock and flour. Non-vegetarians usually add minced white fish or white chicken meat, but for a vegetarian version it can simply be made by combining seasoned beaten egg white with cornflour, vegetarian stock, oil, butter, cream or milk. It is a useful sauce because it can be used on most vegetables, after poaching for a short period in stock, or stir-frying.

Makes 300 ml (½ pint)

4–5 egg whites	4 tbs warm milk
1½ tbs butter	2 tbs cream
1 tbs cornflour	2 tbs vegetable oil
salt and pepper to taste	

Beat the egg whites with a whisk for a minute. Add all the remaining ingredients except oil, and beat them together for a further 1¼ minutes. Heat the vegetable oil in a small pan. When hot, pour in the egg white mixture, and stir vigorously with a wooden spoon for 1½ minutes, and the Fu-Yung sauce is ready for use.

Stir-fried French Beans in Fu-Yung Sauce

This dish presents an attractive green and white mixture. The sauce helps to enrich the vegetable, which after the short cooking should still be crispy. The sauce and the beans make a good dish to go with rice.

Serves 4–5, with other dishes

450 g (1 lb) French beans	1 tbs light soya sauce
2 cloves garlic	½ tsp salt
2 tbs vegetable oil	300 ml (½ pint) Fu-Yung sauce
4 tbs vegetarian stock	(see above)

Top and tail the beans and cut each one in half. Coarsely crush and chop garlic.

Heat oil in a frying pan or wok. When hot, add the beans and garlic, and stir-fry them over medium heat for 2 minutes. Add stock, soya sauce and salt. Continue to stir-fry for 2 minutes, reduce heat, and continue to cook gently until all the liquid has evaporated. Pour in the Fu-Yung sauce. Stir and turn the contents together for a further 1½ minutes.

Stir-fried Courgettes in Fu-Yung Sauce
Serves 4–5, with other dishes

Repeat the previous recipe, using 350g (12oz) courgettes instead of French beans. The courgettes will need to be top and tailed, and cut into 1-cm (½-inch) slices. Otherwise the method is precisely the same, except that, since courgettes are a softer vegetable than French beans, the cooking time after the addition of stock can be shortened by 1 minute.

Fu-Yung Cauliflower with Cheese and Tianjin 'Winter Pickle'
Cauliflower in Fu-Yung sauce is an established dish in China. By adding some grated cheese the dish is further enriched, which should endear it to anyone who enjoys eating rice with a rich savoury sauce.
Serves 4–5, with other dishes

1 large cauliflower	150ml (¼ pint) vegetarian stock
2 tbs winter pickle	1 vegetarian stock cube
2 tbs vegetable oil	300ml (½ pint) Fu-Yung sauce
½ tsp salt	(see page 57)
2 tbs grated cheese	

Cut or break cauliflower into individual florets. Remove the main stem and root. Chop the pickle into loose coarse grains.

Heat oil in a saucepan or wok. When hot, add the pickle and stir around a few times, followed by the cauliflower, sprinkled with salt and cheese. Turn the ingredients round in the pan for half a minute. Pour in the stock and add crumbled stock cube. When it boils, turn the vegetable around gently in the stock for 2 minutes. Reduce heat and cover the pan with a lid. Leave contents to cook gently for 3 minutes. Pour in the Fu-Yung sauce. Turn the vegetable around in the sauce a few times and leave to cook together gently for 2 minutes. Transfer contents into a large serving bowl.

Peking Stir-cooked 'Yellow Running Egg'
This is a well-established Peking dish – another favourite of rice eaters – which in other cuisines might be considered a sauce or semi-soup dish. Diners eat this by spooning the sauce mixture on top of their own bowls of rice, accompanied by other dishes.
Serves 6–7, with other dishes

3 eggs
3 egg yolks
½ tsp salt
1 tbs cornflour
300 ml (½ pint) vegetarian stock
1½ tbs Vesop (or other light vegetarian sauce)
1 cake bean curd
75 g (3 oz) straw mushrooms

2 cloves garlic
2½ tbs butter
2 tbs grated cheese
2½ tbs vegetable oil
3–4 tbs green peas, fresh or frozen
1 tbs light soya sauce
2 tbs chopped coriander leaves or watercress

Beat eggs, egg yolks, half the salt, cornflour, stock and 1 tbs vegetarian sauce with a whisk for 12–15 seconds until the mixture is blended.

Chop and mash the bean curd, drain the mushrooms well. Crush and chop the garlic.

Heat butter in a saucepan. When it has melted, pour in the stock and egg-and-yolk mixture. Stir the mixture with a wooden spoon over medium heat for 2½ minutes. Add salt, remaining ½ tbs Vesop and grated cheese, and continue to stir and mix for a further 2 minutes. Remove from heat.

Heat oil in another saucepan. Add garlic, mushrooms and green peas. Stir them together over medium heat for 1 minute. Add the mashed bean curd and light soya sauce, and continue to stir-fry the ingredients together for a further 2 minutes. Pour in the egg-and-yolk mixture from the other pan. Stir and turn all the ingredients together for a further 2 minutes.

Pour the contents of the pan into a large serving bowl and sprinkle with chopped coriander or watercress.

Steamed Egg Dishes

Basic Steamed Eggs

Chinese steamed eggs could be said to be similar to Western custard, but in effect they are two very different things. Chinese steamed eggs are almost always savoury, and they are usually much lighter (probably because no flour or cornflour is used). Yet, although lighter, they do not flow like cream or thick milk. They are usually made with clear broth, and seldom with more than two eggs beaten into 600 ml (1 pint).

This is an informal dish, but one of some refinement. The steamed eggs are spooned into individual rice bowls and consumed alongside heavier and richer dishes.

Serves 4–5, with other dishes

2 eggs
600 ml (1 pint) good vegetarian
 broth
1 tsp salt
1 tbs Vesop (or any other light
 vegetarian sauce)

1–2 spring onions, cut or
 chopped into fine shavings
1½ tbs soya sauce

Beat eggs with a fork or chopsticks for 10–15 seconds. Add broth, salt and vegetarian sauce. Continue to beat and mix for 10–15 seconds until the mixture is blended.

Pour the egg mixture into a basin or a large ovenproof bowl. Insert the basin or bowl in a steamer and steam vigorously for 15–17 minutes, until the top of the steamed egg has become somewhat firm.

Remove the basin or bowl from the steamer. Sprinkle the top of the steamed egg with chopped spring onion and soya sauce, and serve.

Steamed Eggs with Vegetables and Pickles
Serves 5–6, with other dishes

Repeat the previous recipe, and add 4–5 medium-sized tomatoes (cut into quarters), salt and pepper to taste, 1 tbs chopped 'snow pickle', 1 tbs chopped 'winter pickle', ½ tbs chopped Sichuan Ja Tsai pickle.

Before steaming, pack the tomato pieces at the bottom of the bowl or basin, and sprinkle them with salt and pepper. Pour in the egg mixture so that the tomato is completely submerged. Insert the bowl or basin into a steamer, and steam vigorously for 17–18 minutes. By this time the surface of the egg mixture should have become firm. Sprinkle with the pickles, followed by the chopped spring onion and soya sauce.

Steamed Eggs with Salt Eggs and Hundred-year-old Eggs

The variety of flavours from the three different types of eggs makes this dish quite distinct from any other dish you are likely to encounter.

Serves 5–6, with other dishes

3 hundred-year-old eggs	1 tsp salt
3 salt eggs	1 tbs Vesop or other vegetarian
2 eggs	sauce
450 ml (¾ pint) good vegetarian broth	1–2 spring onions, chopped into fine shavings

Clean and remove the shells from the hundred-year-old eggs. Cut each egg into six equal-wedged sections. Do the same with the salt eggs.

Beat raw eggs with a fork or chopsticks for 10–15 seconds. Add broth, salt and sauce. Continue to beat and mix for 10–15 seconds until the mixture is blended.

Arrange the salt egg and hundred-year-old egg segments over the surface of a large, flat-bottomed, deep-sided heatproof dish. Pour in the beaten egg mixture to half cover the egg pieces. Insert the dish into a steamer, and steam vigorously for 10–12 minutes. Sprinkle the spring onions on top, and serve in the dish in which the eggs have been steamed.

3 Vegetables

Stir-fried Dishes

Quick stir-frying is just beginning to be accepted as a form of cooking in the West although it has been in wide use in China for over two thousand years. It probably became very popular and was accepted as an established form of cooking because of its speed and convenience (it seldom takes more than a couple of minutes to cut foods up into the required size and shapes, and a further 2–3 minutes, or even less, to stir-fry them in a small amount of oil over high heat). With the arrival of the wok in the West in very recent years stir-frying seems to be rapidly catching on, and it has very likely come to stay. Not only is it a very time-saving method of cooking, it is also extremely flexible, capable of producing an almost unlimited range of variations whether in flavour, colour or shape, and in the possible combination of food materials. It is this speed of cooking, the range and flexibility, which makes stir-frying so useful and intriguing.

Stir-frying has another advantage, which is that it is a highly nutritious way of cooking. Since the developed world is getting very health-conscious, it has been explained that, since the cooking time in stir-frying is extremely short, much more of the food's juices and nutrition can be retained. Besides, in stir-frying food materials are cut into small pieces, slices or threads, so many more types of food can be assembled, cooked and presented in one dish. This gives consumers the advantage of drawing nutrition from a greater range of food materials than they would do when customarily confined to eating just one or two, often stodgy, single material bulk-food dishes.

Traditionally, Chinese stir-frying starts by heating no more than 3–4 tbs of oil or fat (for a dish of 3–4 portions, normally served with a couple of other dishes) in a frying pan or wok. When hot, 1–3 tsp of chopped or sliced strong-tasting vegetables, such as onions, spring onions, ginger and garlic are added, individually or mixed, to the hot oil for 10–15 seconds to flavour or season the oil. A small quantity of salt may also be added. When the oil is seasoned the bulk of the principal food material is added to the pan or wok and stir-fried over high heat for 1–1½ minutes during which the pre-chopped, pre-sliced, pre-diced or pre-shredded food material is turned and stirred continuously in the hot oil, and against the hot well-greased metal of the pan. The food should now be two-thirds cooked, and will have released a fair proportion of its natural juices into the pan. At this point the food should be removed with a perforated spoon and put aside for a temporary rest.

The remaining flavoured oil and juices left in the pan (not unlike the flavoured fat left in a normal roasting pan in Western cooking) are quickly made use of to concoct a sauce. This is achieved by adding to the pan or wok a tbs or two of soya sauce (or one of its variants, such as yellow bean paste, hoisin sauce, *tou-pan* chilli-soya paste), chicken stock, wine and a tsp or two of sugar (to enrich the sauce). When these ingredients are stirred together in the pan or wok they immediately start to combine, boil and froth up. A small amount of blended cornflour (about 2 tsp cornflour blended in 1½–2 tbs water) is now introduced to thicken the sauce. At this point the partially cooked principal food material is returned to the wok, stirred and coated in the sauce. The turning and stirring over high heat need not last for longer than a further ½–1 minute when the dish should be deemed cooked. A tsp of sesame oil and 2 tsp of freshly chopped chives or spring onion, are frequently sprinkled over the food just before serving to enhance its aromatic appeal. This whole process of stir-frying does not normally last for much more than 3–3½ minutes, depending on the quantity of the food to be cooked, the size of the pan or wok used (the bigger, the quicker), the level of heat used, and the size and thickness of the cut foods.

Hence, in Chinese stir-fry cooking, timing and 'heat control' are of paramount importance, and these can only be achieved by having served time over the cooker. But the skill of stir-frying can be acquired, and all the mystique which surrounds the subject forgotten. Since every dish prepared may require special attention and finesse to cook it to perfection, and since in Chinese cooking stir-fried dishes run into hundreds or thousands, it will require time to cover the mileage. But it should be encouraging to know that the basic skill, or even a feeling of mastery, can be achieved over the cooker in no more than a dozen sessions. However, a good deal of eating experience, and a knowledge of the range of Chinese cuisine, is important in order to know what should actually be aimed for in any particular Chinese stir-fried dish. What is normally desired is a happy balance of the sweet freshness of the food and its juices, and the matured flavour of the seasonings and flavouring agents employed. Harmony is achieved when the two sides are perfectly balanced, especially when the elements of textural and colour appeal are conspicuous in the final presentation of the dish.

Through the permutation of food materials and flavouring ingredients used, the number of dishes which can be prepared by stir-frying is almost unlimited. What I shall aim to do in this chapter is to provide recipes which illustrate how some of the popular vegetables are traditionally cooked on their own, or together, in the traditional manner – and thus provide some guidelines as to how to go about stir-frying these vegetables without indulging myself in writing out innumerable recipes to impress readers with the scope and scale of Chinese vegetable cookery.

Stir-fried Bean Sprouts with Garlic and Spring Onions
Since bean sprouts require no cutting, and are quite edible whether cooked or not, this is one of the easiest and most convenient vegetable dishes to cook.
Serves 3–4, with 1–2 other dishes

450g (1lb) bean sprouts	1½tbs vegetarian stock
3–4 cloves garlic	1tbs light soya sauce
3 spring onions	1tbs vinegar
3½tbs vegetable oil	1½tsp sesame oil
1tsp salt	

Wash and shake the sprouts thoroughly in water. Dry well. Crush garlic, and coarsely chop. Cut spring onions into 6-mm (¼-inch) shavings (separating white parts from the green).

Heat oil in a large frying pan or wok. When hot, add salt, garlic and the whites of the spring onions, and stir them around in the hot oil for 15 seconds. Add the sprouts, and turn and stir them together with the other ingredients over high heat for 1 minute. Sprinkle the contents with stock, soya sauce and vinegar. Continue to stir-fry over high heat for a further minute. Sprinkle contents with the greens of the spring onion and sesame oil. Stir, turn once more and serve.

Stir-fried French Beans with Garlic and Chinese Dried Mushrooms
The seasoned oil developed from the garlic, mushroom, stock, 'cheese', soya and sherry to coat the beans should make the latter extremely flavoursome, and ideal to consume with quantities of plain cooked rice.
Serves 3–4, with 1–2 other dishes

450g (1lb) young French beans	1½tbs light soya sauce
3 cloves garlic	1tbs sherry
3–4 Chinese dried mushrooms	4½tbs vegetable oil
2tsp Chinese red bean curd	1tsp salt
'cheese'	1½tsp sesame oil
3tbs vegetarian stock	

Top and tail the beans, and cut each piece into halves. Crush and coarsely chop the garlic. Soak dried mushrooms in boiling water for half an hour. Remove and discard stems, and coarsely chop caps. Blend bean curd 'cheese' with stock, soya sauce and sherry.

Heat 3½ tbs oil in a frying pan or wok. When hot, add salt, garlic and chopped mushrooms. Stir them in the hot oil for half a minute. Add the beans, and stir and turn in the seasoned oil with the dried mushroom and garlic for 2 minutes. Add the 'cheese', stock, soya and sherry mixture. Turn them with the beans quickly over high heat for a further 2 minutes. Sprinkle contents with remainder of oil, and sesame oil. Turn and stir once more and serve.

Stir-fried Young Cabbage with Root-ginger and Snow Pickles

Although flavoursome and savoury, the cabbage is full of wholesome vegetable flavour and still crispy to the bite. Cooked like this, the cabbage can be consumed in quantity on its own, or with rice and other dishes.

Serves 4–5, with 1–2 other dishes

1 young savoy cabbage 700 g– 1 kg (about 1½–2 lb)	1 tsp salt
	4–5 tbs vegetarian stock
3 slices root-ginger	1 tbs wine vinegar
2 tbs snow pickle	2 tbs light soya sauce
4½ tbs vegetable oil	1½ tsp sesame oil

Remove the outer leaves of the cabbage, cut away and discard its stem. Cut the tenderer parts of the cabbage into thin slices. Coarsely chop ginger and pickle.

Heat oil in a large frying pan or wok. When hot, add salt, ginger and pickle. Stir them in the hot oil for half a minute. Add the cabbage, and stir and turn quickly with other ingredients in the seasoned oil over medium heat for 2 minutes. Add the stock, vinegar and soya sauce. Continue to turn and stir the ingredients together for 1½ minutes. Spread the cabbage evenly over the pan, and leave to cook for a further 1 minute. Turn and scramble the ingredients together, and leave to cook for a further minute. Sprinkle with sesame oil, and serve. The cabbage should now look glistening green on a white serving dish.

Stir-fried Hot and Sour Chinese Cabbage
Another boon for rice-eaters, who enjoy sharp-tasting foods with the
blandness of plain cooked rice.
Serves 3–4, with 1–2 other dishes

Repeat the previous recipe, but substitute Chinese cabbage
(sometimes called Chinese leaves) for savoy cabbage, use 2 red
chilli peppers and 1 dried chilli pepper instead of pickles, and
increase the quantity of vinegar used from 1 tbs to 2½ tbs.
Adopt the same cooking procedure, adding shredded peppers
(after discarding pips) into the hot oil to stir-fry for half a
minute, before adding the bulk of the cabbage. The resultant
dish will be slightly pink in colour, and should appeal to all
those who enjoy spicy food.

Sweet and Sour Cabbage
This is another appealing dish to have with rice. Either sweet or
savoy cabbage can be used. For those who enjoy spicy food, ½ tbs
chilli sauce may be added to the ingredients for the sauce.
Serves 4–5, with other dishes

700 g–1 kg (1½–2 lb) cabbage
2 slices root-ginger
4 tbs vegetable oil
1 tsp salt
4 tbs vegetarian stock
Sauce:
2 tbs sugar

3½ tbs wine vinegar
1½ tbs light soya sauce
1½ tbs tomato purée
2 tbs orange juice
1 tbs cornflour blended in 3 tbs
    water

Cut cabbage into thin slices, after removing outer leaves and
discarding the stem. Cut ginger into fine shreds, and mix the
ingredients for the sauce until well blended.

Heat oil in a large frying pan or wok. When hot, add the
shredded ginger and salt to stir in the hot oil for quarter of a
minute. Add the bulk of cabbage to stir and turn in the
seasoned oil until every piece is well coated and lubricated.
Spread the cabbage evenly over the pan or wok. Sprinkle it
evenly with stock. As the stock bubbles and froths, turn and
stir the cabbage over high heat for 1½ minutes. Mix together
the sauce ingredients and pour evenly over the pan. Stir and

turn the cabbage over a few times, until the sauce begins to thicken, and becomes glistening and glossy.

Stir-fried Spinach with Garlic and Chinese Bean Curd 'Cheese'

Although a simple dish by ordinary culinary standards, it often turns out to be the most appealing on the menu of any reputable restaurant in China or abroad. What makes it appealing is the unmistakable character and quality of the vegetable cooked and eaten in bulk.
Serves 3–4, with 1–2 other dishes

450 g (1 lb) young spinach	½ tbs bean curd 'cheese'
4 cloves garlic	1 tbs light soya sauce
4½ tbs vegetable oil	1 tsp sesame oil
1 tsp salt	

Wash and dry spinach thoroughly. Remove and discard stems, and any discoloured leaves. Cut spinach into 2.5-cm (1-inch) slices. Crush and coarsely chop garlic.

Heat 4 tbs oil in a large frying pan or wok. When hot, add garlic and salt and stir them over medium heat for quarter of a minute. Add 'cheese', and stir and mix the ingredients together for another half minute. Add the bulk of the spinach into the pan and turn and mix evenly with the garlic, 'cheese' and seasoned oil. Continue to turn and mix over medium heat for 1½ minutes. Add soya sauce, remaining oil and sesame oil. Stir and turn for half a minute over high heat and serve.

Stir-fried Asparagus with Garlic

The asparagus should be bright green, glistening and still crunchy when served. The appeal of this dish lies in the fullness of the distinctive vegetable flavour when eaten in mouthfuls.
Serves 3–4, with 1–2 other dishes

450–550 g (1–1¼ lb) young asparagus	1½ tsp sugar
	1 tbs soya sauce
2 cloves garlic	3 tbs vegetarian stock
4½ tbs vegetable oil	1 tbs dry sherry
1 tsp salt	

Remove and discard the tough root-end of the asparagus stems. Cut each piece into halves. Cut the white lower end of the asparagus slantwise in 1.5-cm (⅔-inch) sections, and the spears into 5-cm (2-inch) sections. Parboil the white sections in boiling water for 5–6 minutes and drain. Crush and coarsely chop garlic.

Heat oil in a frying pan or wok. When hot, add salt, garlic and asparagus. Turn them in the hot oil over high heat for 2 minutes. Add sugar, soya sauce, stock and sherry. Stir and turn the vegetable over in the sauce several times. Reduce heat to low, and spread the vegetable evenly over the pan. Leave to cook for 3–3½ minutes until all the liquid has evaporated. Stir, turn once more, and serve.

Stir-fried Broccoli with Garlic

This is another green, crunchy, vegetable dish very similar to the previous one in appearance and appeal. The sweet, fresh vegetable taste is made more apparent by being contrasted with the sauce's savoury saltiness.
Serves 3–4, with 1–2 other dishes

450–550 g (1–1¼ lb) broccoli	1 tbs dry sherry
2 cloves garlic	3½ tbs vegetable oil
2 tsp bean curd 'cheese'	1 tsp salt
2½ tbs vegetarian stock	1½ tsp sugar
1 tbs soya sauce	

Remove the lower roots of the broccoli, and cut the stems slantwise into 2-cm (¾-inch) slices. Parboil them in boiling water for 2 minutes and drain well. Break the florets into individual 2.5–4-cm (1–1½-inch) florets. Crush and coarsely chop garlic. Mix the 'cheese' with the stock, soya sauce and sherry until well blended.

Heat oil in a frying pan or wok. When hot, add the salt and garlic. Stir them around for 20 seconds, and add both the sliced stems and florets of the broccoli. Stir and turn them around in the hot oil with the garlic for 1 minute, until every piece of vegetable is well coated by the seasoned oil. Pour the mixture of soya-stock-sherry-cheese over the broccoli after sprinkling it with sugar. Turn and stir the sauce until every piece of vegetable is evenly covered. Réduce heat to low and leave contents to cook gently for 2½ minutes. Turn and stir once more, and serve.

Mixed Vegetable Dishes

These are just a few examples of the many familiar combinations.

Stir-fried Lima (or Fava) Beans with Straw Mushrooms

A very satisfying dish to spoon into your rice bowl and eat with mouthfuls of rice. Serve in a deep-sided dish or a serving bowl.
Serves 5–6, with other dishes

225–300 g (8–10 oz) fresh or
   frozen lima beans
175–225 g (6–8 oz) canned straw
   mushrooms
4–4½ tbs vegetable oil
1 tsp salt

½ tsp sugar
¾ tbs light soya sauce
1½ tsp sesame oil
2½ tsp cornflour blended in
   2 tbs water

Parboil the beans in boiling water for 2½–3 minutes and drain. Drain the straw mushrooms (reserving 4 tbs mushroom water).

Heat oil in saucepan or wok. When hot, add the beans and stir-fry them over medium heat for 2 minutes. Add the straw mushrooms, salt and sugar, and stir-fry them together for 1½ minutes. Add soya sauce, 4 tbs mushroom water and the sesame oil. Stir and turn all the ingredients together for a further 2 minutes. Finally add the blended cornflour. Continue mixing and turning until the sauce thickens and turns somewhat translucent.

Stir-fried Fava Beans with Pickles

The majority of Chinese dishes of this type are calculated for consuming with rice. In this case the richness of the purée gives body to the dish, and the quantity of oil in the dish provides the 'lubrication' necessary when eating quantities of rice.
Serves 4–5, with 1–2 other dishes

150–175 g (5–6 oz) dried fava
   beans or dried split green
   peas
4 tbs snow pickle
1½ tbs Sichuan hot Ja Tsai
   pickle

75–100 g (3–4 oz) bean sprouts
4 tbs vegetable oil
1 tsp sugar
1½ tsp sesame oil
1 tbs soya sauce

Soak beans (or peas) overnight in cold water. Rinse under
running water. Place them in a saucepan and bring to boil.
Simmer gently for 40–45 minutes. Reserve 150 ml (¼ pint) of
the water, and drain. Coarsely chop both types of pickles.
Mash beans (or peas) into a purée, cut bean sprouts into
6-mm (¼-inch) shavings.

   Heat 1½ tbs oil in a saucepan or wok. When hot, add the
pickles and stir-fry for 1 minute. Add the remaining oil and
sugar, followed by the vegetable purée. Stir over low-medium
heat for 1½ minutes. Pour in the reserved stock and sprouts
and continue to stir and mix for 2½ minutes. Add sesame oil
and soya sauce and continue to cook and stir gently for a
further half minute before serving.

Stir-fried Courgettes with Braised Bamboo Shoots and Button Mushrooms

The combined effect of braised bamboo shoots, pickle and chilli
should give this dish a pronounced savoury flavour, making it
another favourite for rice-eaters.
Serves 4–5, with 1–2 other dishes

350 g (12 oz) courgettes
225 g (8 oz) braised bamboo
   shoots (available canned and
   marinated)
225 g (8 oz) button mushrooms
2 tbs snow pickle

2 small dried chillies
4 tbs vegetable oil
1 tbs light soya sauce
3 tbs vegetarian stock
1½ tsp sesame oil

Top and tail the courgettes, and cut each slantwise into
sections 1 cm (½ inch) thick. Cut bamboo shoots into
similar-sized pieces. Clean mushrooms and cut through stalk
and cap into halves. Chop the pickle and chillies (discarding
pips).

Heat oil in a frying pan or work. When hot, add the pickles and chillies. Stir-fry them in the hot oil for 1 minute. Add the bamboo shoots, courgettes and mushrooms. Continue to stir-fry over medium heat for 3 minutes. Add the soya sauce and stock, which should start to boil and bubble immediately. Stir and turn the ingredients in the bubbling sauce for 1 more minute, add sesame oil and serve.

Stir-fried Snow Peas (Mangetouts) with Baby Corn, Dried Mushrooms and 'Tree-ear' Fungi

This is a colourful dish with the bright green of the mangetouts, the blackness of the tree fungi and dried mushrooms, and the yellowness of the baby corn, all contrasting sharply in colour and texture.
Serves 5–6, with 1–2 other dishes

225 g (8 oz) mangetouts	2 tsp bean curd 'cheese'
150–175 g (5–6 oz) canned baby corn	2 tbs vegetarian stock
	3½ tbs vegetable oil
4–5 medium-sized Chinese dried mushrooms	¾ tsp salt
	1 tsp sugar
2 slices root-ginger	1 tbs light soya sauce
3–4 tbs dried 'tree-ear' fungi	1 tbs dry sherry

Trim and cut each mangetout slantwise into halves. Drain the baby corn. Soak dried mushrooms in boiling water for half an hour. Remove stems, and cut each cap into quarters. Shred the ginger. Soak the tree ears for 4–5 minutes, rinse, wash and drain. Mix 'cheese' with stock until well blended.

Heat oil in a frying pan or wok. When hot, add ginger and mushrooms and stir-fry together for 1 minute, followed by the mangetouts, salt and tree ears. Stir and turn them together over medium heat for 1½ minutes. Add baby corn and sugar, then pour in the soya sauce, sherry and the 'cheese'-stock mixture. This should immediately froth up into a bubbling sauce mixture. Turn the contents quickly in the sauce over high heat and stir constantly for 1½ more minutes. By this time most of the moisture will have evaporated, and the sauce will have formed a savoury coating on the vegetables.

Braised Chinese Vegetable Dishes

Much more use seems to be made of the stems of vegetables in Chinese cooking than in Western. When vegetable stems are cooked with care they can often be just as appealing and palatable, if not even more satisfying, than the leaves and tops of vegetables. In the majority of cases the stems require longer cooking to tenderize than could be achieved through a couple of minutes of stir-frying. Hence the cooking method most often used in cooking hard roots or stems is *braising*.

In China, braising can be a simple continuation of the stir-frying process where some stock and sauce are added and the heat reduced so that the vegetable can be cooked slowly, partly in its own juice, and partly in the stock and sauce added. It may be 10–12 minutes before the vegetable is tender.

Braising also involves cooking the harder vegetables along with flavouring ingredients, such as pickles, dried ingredients and sauces, over a gentle heat for a good period of time (20–30 minutes). This results in the chunkier cuts of vegetables being 'dry cooked' (rather like pot roasting) until tenderized and made flavoursome by the slow action of the added sauces and the lengthy cooking of the vegetables in their own juices.

Effective braising can also be achieved by cooking hard vegetables over high heat in ample sauce and stock through a process of rapid reduction. When nearly all the moisture and liquid have evaporated, after 20 minutes or more of vigorous boiling or stewing, the vegetables will have become suitably tenderized and coated by a sauce, the ingredients for which can be varied and made up as the cooking proceeds.

Whichever process is used, braised vegetables can be used extensively in stir-frying with the tenderer-leaf (or quick-cooked) vegetables to produce a whole new range of vegetable dishes. This is more or less how Chinese dishes multiply, giving rise to new horizons which seem to be never ending.

Most people are aware of the pleasure of eating the leaves of fresh, crispy vegetables, but few have achieved the cultivated taste and enjoyment of biting into a thick chunk of crunchy vegetable such as a wedge of triangularly cut turnip, carrot or bamboo shoot, when the teeth sink through the outer surface of the chunky vegetable made savoury by the long period of cooking in a sauce. Most Chinese gastronomes have gained this cultivated taste from eating all different types of bamboo shoots: winter bamboo shoots, bamboo-shoot tips, chunky bamboo shoots, pickled bamboo shoots, soya-braised marinated bamboo shoots, and so on.

This inevitably extended to all other thick, crunchy vegetables, such as carrots, turnips, asparagus, broccoli and cauliflower stems, parsnips, marrows, winter melons, cucumbers and celery. These vegetables are cooked in different ways (some soya-braised with or without sugar and chilli; others simmered in stock, or quickly stir-fried), but all are thick-cut into varying shapes and sizes, to be cooked together with leaf vegetables, noodles or transparent pea- or bean-starch noodles (which can withstand lengthy cooking without becoming mushy). A whole genre of dishes consequently stems from the many possible combinations.

Normally in Chinese cooking the cutting of supplementary ingredients should follow the shape and size of the principal ingredient of the dish (so that in the cooking of a noodle dish, for example, the supplementary ingredients and materials should all be cut into thin strips like noodles). In some cases, however, materials and ingredients are purposely left, or cut into contrasting sizes and shapes, to provide variation – especially when such ingredients or materials are able to retain much of their original flavour because of their thickness. These larger cuts of chunky vegetables, cooked in varying ways and for different lengths of time, therefore have their special function in the ever-varying combination of materials and ingredients characteristic of Chinese cooking.

Mixed Stir-fry of 'Two Winters' with Courgettes

This is both a very tasty and crunchy dish, which can be eaten as a starter, as a snack accompanied by wine, or eaten with plain rice.

Serves 4–5, with 1–2 other dishes

100–150 g (4–5 oz) winter bamboo shoots	¾ tsp salt
	1 tsp sugar
6 large Chinese dried winter mushrooms	3 tbs vegetarian stock
	1 tbs light soya sauce
1½ medium-sized courgettes	1 tbs dry sherry
3½ tbs vegetable oil	1 tbs margarine or butter
3 slices root-ginger	1 tbs sesame oil

Cut bamboo shoots into 4–4.5-cm (1½–1¾-inch) triangular wedged pieces. Soak dried mushrooms in boiling water for half an hour. Remove the stems and cut caps into quarters (retaining 3 tbs mushroom water). Remove the ends of the courgettes, and cut slantwise into 1-cm (½-inch) slices.

Heat oil in a frying pan or wok. When hot, add ginger and mushrooms. Stir-fry them over high heat for 1 minute. Add bamboo shoots, salt, sugar, mushroom water and stock. Continue to turn and stir for 1 minute. Place a lid over the pan or wok, reduce heat and leave contents to cook gently for 2 minutes. Add courgettes, soya sauce, sherry and margarine or butter. Stir-fry all the ingredients together for a further 1½ minutes. Sprinkle with sesame oil and serve.

Stir-fry of Two Braised and Two Simmered Shredded Vegetables

One of the enjoyments of eating this dish is the multitexture and multiflavour sensation it gives when biting through the strands and threads of the four different vegetables.

Serves 4–5, with other dishes

2 medium-sized young carrots	3 tbs vegetable oil
100–150 g (4–5 oz) bamboo shoots	1 tsp sugar
	1 tbs yellow bean sauce
3 slices root-ginger	4 tbs vegetarian stock
3 medium-sized dried mushrooms	1 tbs soya sauce
	1 tbs margarine or butter
2 sticks celery	1 tsp sesame oil
15-cm (6-inch) section medium-sized cucumber	

Clean and cut carrots, bamboo shoots and ginger into match-stick shreds. Soak mushrooms in boiling water for half an hour (retaining water). Remove stems, and cut caps into similar shreds. Clean and cut celery and cucumber into double matchstick strips.

Heat oil in a frying pan or wok. When hot, add ginger and mushrooms and stir-fry over high heat for 1 minute. Add carrots, bamboo shoots, mushroom water, sugar and yellow bean sauce. Turn and stir the ingredients. Reduce heat and leave contents to braise and simmer together for 3 minutes, turning them over now and then.

Heat stock and soya sauce together in a pan or wok. When the mixture boils, add the celery and cucumber. Turn them in the sauce, and leave them to simmer for 2 minutes – by which time the liquid in the pan or wok should nearly have dried up.

Transfer the contents of the second pan or wok into the first. Add the margarine or butter and sesame oil. Stir-fry the contents together for a further 1 minute, and serve.

Four Soya-braised Chunky Vegetables with Pickles

This is a dish of rich, glistening, chunky vegetables, often used in China to nibble, chew and crunch in the mouth, while drinking wine; or it can also be consumed with plain boiled rice.
Serves 4–5, with other dishes

2 large young carrots	1½ tbs yellow bean sauce
100 g (4 oz) turnips	1½ tbs soya sauce
100 g (4 oz) parsnips	2 tsp chilli sauce
100 g (4 oz) bamboo shoots	150 ml (¼ pint) vegetarian stock
1½ tbs snow pickle	1 tbs dry sherry
1 tbs Ja Tsai pickle	1 tbs margarine or butter
4 tbs vegetable oil	1½ tsp sesame oil
1 tbs sugar	1½ tbs chopped parsley

Scrape, clean and cut carrots, turnips and parsnips into 4–5-cm (1½–2-inch) triangular wedged pieces. Cut bamboo shoots into similar-sized and shaped pieces. Coarsely chop pickles.

Heat oil in a heavy saucepan or casserole. When hot, add the pickles and stir them in the hot oil for half a minute. Add all the vegetables, and stir and turn in the seasoned oil for 1 minute. Add sugar, yellow bean sauce, soya sauce, chilli sauce and stock. Bring contents to boil, and turn around a few times. Cover the pan or casserole with a lid. Reduce heat and leave contents to braise and simmer for 5–6 minutes. Remove the lid and turn the contents over several times. Cover again and allow the contents to braise and simmer for a further 5–6 minutes. Remove the lid once more and add the sherry, margarine or butter and sesame oil. Raise heat to high, and stir-fry the contents until nearly all the sauce which coats the vegetables has thickened to a glaze. Sprinkle contents with chopped parsley and serve.

Sichuan Hot-braised Stir-fried Aubergine

This is a hot spicy dish, typical of the province of Sichuan, and most suitable for eating with copious amounts of plain boiled rice. Most of these provincial dishes are 'dishes for the masses', which are meant for hearty eating. But over the years they have assumed a refined and classical status.
Serves 4–5, with other dishes

2 medium-sized aubergines	4 tbs vegetarian stock
2 slices root-ginger	1 tbs soya sauce
3–4 dried red chillies	1½ tbs chilli-bean paste
2 spring onions	1½ tbs wine vinegar
4 tbs vegetable oil	2½ tsp cornflour blended in
1½ tbs yellow bean sauce	2 tbs water
2 tsp sugar	1 tsp sesame oil
½ tsp salt	

Remove the stem ends of the aubergines. Cut aubergines into strips approximately 1 × 1 × 6 cm (½ × ½ × 2½ inches). Shred the ginger, and coarsely chop chillies after removing pips and stalk. Cuit spring onions into 6-mm (¼-inch) shavings (separating the whites and greens).

Heat oil in a wok or heavy saucepan. When hot, add ginger, chillies and the whites of the spring onion. Stir-fry them together for 1 minute. Add yellow bean sauce, sugar, salt, stock and aubergine. Raise heat to high, turn and stir the contents together in the bubbling sauce for 1½ minutes. Reduce heat to low and leave contents to simmer gently under cover for 3 minutes. Remove the lid and add soya sauce, chilli-bean paste and vinegar. Stir and turn them over high heat for 1 minute. Pour in the blended cornflour. Stir and turn to mix in with other ingredients in the pan or wok. As soon as the blended cornflour thickens and turns translucent, sprinkle with the greens of the spring onion and sesame oil and serve.

Stir-fried Transparent Bean-starch Noodles with Lily Buds, Mushrooms, 'Tree Fungi' and Braised Stems of Broccoli and Heart of Cabbage

Bean-starch transparent noodles are a great absorber of liquid. Their weight is increased at least four times when soaked in water. However, unlike wheat-starch noodles, they are not eaten as bulk food, or on their own, but usually as a supplementary ingredient for cooking with other food materials. As such, and because of its equal ability to absorb the flavours of other ingredients, it plays a unique part in augmenting savoury dishes and providing bulk dishes to accompany rice (for example, by adding gravy to transparent noodles a dish of considerable dimension and savouriness can be created and at very little cost, which can be as appealing as another dish which may cost ten times as much). It is a dish which is often seen on family dining tables.

Serves 5–6, with other dishes

75–100 g (3–4 oz) dry transparent noodles	90 g (3½ oz) broccoli stems
2 lily buds	90 g (3½ oz) heart and stem of cabbage
3 tbs 'tree fungi'	3½ tbs vegetable oil
2 slices root-ginger	1 tsp salt
6 medium-sized dried mushrooms	300 ml (½ pint) vegetarian stock
2 tbs snow pickle	1 tbs soya sauce
2 tbs winter pickle	1 vegetarian stock cube
	1 tsp sesame oil

Soak noodles and lily buds in warm water for 5 minutes and drain. Cut lily buds into 4-cm (1½-inch) sections. Soak fungi in warm water for 3 minutes. Wash under running water, and cut into roughly 5-cm (2-inch) pieces. Shred ginger. Soak mushrooms in boiling water for half an hour, remove stems, and cut caps into matchstick shreds. Coarsely chop the pickles. Cut broccoli and cabbage into nice neat 4 × 1-cm (1½ × ½-inch) pieces.

Heat oil in a saucepan or wok. When hot, add ginger, dried mushrooms, salt, lily buds and pickles. Stir them over medium heat for 1½ minutes. Add the noodles, and stir and turn them with the other ingredients in the seasoned oil for 2½ minutes.

Meanwhile, heat stock in a separate pan or wok. When it begins to boil, add the broccoli stems and heart of cabbage. When contents reboil, add soya sauce and crumbled stock cube. Reduce heat and allow the contents to simmer gently together for 5 minutes, or until half of the liquid has evaporated.

Transfer the contents of the second pan or wok into the first. Raise heat to high. Turn and stir all ingredients together for 2½ minutes. Sprinkle with sesame oil and serve.

Stir-fried and Braised Asparagus Tips with Bamboo-shoot Spears and Ready-soya-braised Bamboo Shoots and Snow Pickle

With the principal ingredients of this dish only needing to be cooked for a short time, it is highly crunchy and should appeal to the texturally conscious gastronome. In China this is a dish which is frequently used to entertain wine drinkers.
Serves 5–6, with other dishes

3 slices root-ginger
450 g (1 lb) fresh young
  asparagus
225 g (8 oz) bamboo-shoot
  spears
150 g (5 oz) canned ready-
  braised bamboo shoots
3 tbs vegetable oil
2 tbs Sichuan Ja Tsai pickle

3 tbs snow pickle
½ tsp salt
2 tsp sugar
150 ml (¼ pint) vegetarian stock
1 tbs yellow bean sauce
2 tsp bean curd 'cheese'
1½ tbs dry sherry

Cut root-ginger into shreds. Remove and discard the tough coarser end of the asparagus stems. Cut the tip end into approximately 7.5-cm (3-inch) lengths. Cut bamboo-shoot spears and braised bamboo shoots into approximately the same lengths.

Heat oil in a large frying pan or wok. When hot, add the ginger, pickle and salt, and stir them in the hot oil for half a minute. Add the asparagus and stir in the seasoned oil with other ingredients for 1 minute. Add the bamboo-shoot spears and sugar, and pour in the stock. Bring contents to the boil, reduce heat and leave contents to cook gently for 3–4 minutes. Add braised bamboo shoots, turn the contents over several times and leave to simmer together for a further 2 minutes. By this time the liquid in the pan or wok should have been reduced to less than one quarter. Add the yellow bean sauce, bean curd 'cheese' and sherry. Raise heat to high, and turn and stir the contents over high heat for 1 more minute, which should further reduce the sauce to a mere glaze.

Braised Red-cooked Cabbage

This dish should be served in a deep-sided dish or a large bowl. It is highly savoury, and because of its sweet appealing flavour, people are inclined to eat more vegetable than they normally do. The oil and fat combine to add to the succulence of the dish.
Serves 5–6, with other dishes

1 medium-sized white cabbage (about 1–1.5 kg/2–3 lb)	2 tbs light soya sauce
	1½ tbs dark soya sauce
3 slices root-ginger	1 tbs sugar
4 tbs vegetable oil	1½ tbs margarine or butter
4 tbs vegetarian stock	

Remove the tough lower stem of the cabbage. Cut cabbage first into slices 2.5 cm (1 inch) thick, and then further cut into 5-cm (2-inch) pieces. Shred ginger.

Heat oil in a heavy saucepan or casserole. Add ginger and stir in the hot oil for half a minute. Add all the cabbage and turn in the seasoned oil over medium heat for 1 minute. Add stock, soya sauce and sugar. Continue to stir and turn the contents for 1 minute. Cover the pan or casserole, and reduce heat to low. Leave to simmer for 5 minutes. Remove the lid, add the margarine or butter, and turn and stir the contents once more to see that the cabbage is evenly sauced and 'lubricated'. Allow the contents to simmer gently for a further 5 minutes. By this time the cabbage should be sufficiently cooked. It should have become both rich and tender, although some parts will remain appealingly crunchy.

White-cooked Cabbage

This is another highly savoury dish. As in the previous recipe, it should be served in a deep-sided dish or a large bowl. Because of the succulence of the dish and its rich vegetable flavour, it is ideal for consuming with rice, and it encourages people to eat cabbage in quantity with enjoyment.

Serves 5–6, with other dishes

1 medium-sized white or Chinese Tientsin cabbage (about 1.25–1.5 kg/2½–3 lb)	1½ tsp salt
	4 tbs vegetarian stock
2 slices root-ginger	1 tbs light soya sauce
1 tbs Sichuan hot Ja Tsai pickle	1 vegetarian stock cube
2 red chillies	4 tbs milk
4 tbs vegetable oil	1½ tbs margarine or butter

Remove the tougher lower stem of the cabbage. Cut cabbage first into slices 2.5 cm (1 inch) thick, and then into 5-cm (2-inch) pieces. Shred ginger, pickle and pepper (discarding pulp and pips).

Heat oil in saucepan or casserole. Add ginger, pepper and pickle. Stir them in the hot oil for 1 minute. Add the cabbage, salt, stock and soya sauce. Stir and turn them together over medium heat for 1½ minutes, or until all the vegetable is well sauced and 'lubricated'. Cover the pan or casserole and leave contents to cook gently over low heat for 5 minutes. Remove the lid and add crumbled stock cube, milk and margarine. Stir and turn the contents so as to mix the ingredients evenly. Replace the lid and leave the contents to simmer gently for a further 5 minutes.

Stir-fried Semi-soup Dishes

This is a distinct category of dish in Chinese cuisine, and one which is seldom seen in Western cooking. The main reason for this is because Chinese meals are centred around rice, which is made easier and more appealing to eat by the ample provision of sauce and savoury soup dishes.

Preparing these dishes usually starts with stir-frying. The Chinese believe that it is necessary to cook dried, pickled, salted or strong-tasting ingredients in hot oil first, in order to 'liberate' their flavours; and that it is only after the flavours have been 'liberated' that the other ingredients and materials should be added to produce the bulk of the dish. The following few recipes should illustrate this method.

Stir-fried Semi-soup Dish of Mushrooms, Pickles, Cucumber and Cabbage
Serve in a deep-sided dish or large bowl. This is a rich vegetable dish, suitable for eating with copious amounts of rice.
Serves 5–6, with other dishes

1½ tbs dried salted turnips (Lo Po Kan)
75 g (3 oz) braised and marinated bamboo shoots
15-cm (6-inch) section medium-sized cucumber
225 g (8 oz) Chinese Tientsin cabbage
75 g (3 oz) baby corn (available canned)
4–6 medium-sized Chinese dried mushrooms
3½ tbs vegetable oil

1½ tbs Sichuan hot Ja Tsai pickle, shredded
1½ tbs snow pickle, chopped
2 tbs winter pickle, ready shredded
300 ml (½ pint) vegetarian stock
1 vegetarian stock cube
75 g (3 oz) bean sprouts
1 tsp salt
1 tbs light soya sauce
1½ tsp sesame oil
2 tbs coriander leaves, chopped

Shred the turnips. Cut braised bamboo shoots into 5-cm (2-inch) sections, and cucumber (including skin) into similar-sized pieces. Cut cabbage into slices 1 cm (½ inch) thick, drain the baby corn. Soak mushrooms in boiling water, remove stems and cut caps into shreds.

Heat oil in a saucepan or casserole. When hot, add the pickles and mushrooms. Stir-fry them together for 1½ minutes over medium heat. Add bamboo shoots, turnip and cabbage, and pour in the stock. Bring contents to boil, add crumbled stock cube and simmer them together for 5 minutes. Add bean sprouts, cucumber, baby corn, salt and soya sauce. Turn and stir them together, and continue to cook gently for 5 minutes. Sprinkle with sesame oil and chopped coriander leaves, and serve.

Stir-fried Semi-soup Dish of Mushrooms, Pickles, Braised Bamboo Shoots, Broccoli, Transparent Noodles and Seaweed
Serves 5–6, with other dishes

4–5 medium-sized dried mushrooms
2 tbs snow pickle
100–150 g (3–5 oz) broccoli or broccoli stems
75–100 g (3–4 oz) braised bamboo shoots
50 g (2 oz) dried kelp (Hai Tai, available from Chinese foodstores)
25 g (1 oz) hair seaweed (Fa Tsai, available from Chinese foodstores)

75 g (3 oz) dry transparent bean-starch noodles
3½ tbs vegetable oil
300 ml (½ pint) vegetarian stock
1 vegetarian stock cube
50–75 g (2–3 oz) bean sprouts
1 tsp salt
1½ tbs light soya sauce
2–3 sheets purple seaweed (Tze Tsai, available from Chinese foodstores)
1 tsp sesame oil

Soak mushrooms in boiling water for half an hour, remove stems and shred caps. Coarsely chop pickle. Cut broccoli or broccoli stems and bamboo shoots into 4 × 1-cm (1½ × ½-inch) sections. Soak kelp for 15 minutes, drain and cut into 5 × 1-cm (2 × ½-inch) strips. Soak hair seaweed and noodles for 5 minutes and drain.

Heat oil in a large saucepan or casserole. When hot, add mushrooms, pickle and braised bamboo shoots. Stir them in the hot oil for 1½ minutes. Add broccoli and kelp and stir all the ingredients together for a further 1½ minutes. Pour in the stock, add crumbled stock cube, noodles, bean sprouts, hair seaweed, salt and soya sauce. Stir them all together, and bring contents to boil. Reduce heat, and simmer gently for a further 5–6 minutes. Serve in a deep-sided dish or large bowl. Sprinkle the top of the dish with crumbled purple seaweed and sesame oil.

Stir-fried Semi-soup Dish of Mushrooms, Cucumber, Bamboo Shoots, Asparagus Spears, Winter Melon, Green Peas, Transparent Noodles and Bean Sprouts, Served in a Melon Bowl (Tung Kua Chung)

This is quite a classic dish which is usually served at a party meal. By serving the dish in a natural vegetable bowl it doubly emphasizes the vegetarian nature of the dish.
Serve with other dishes for a party meal

Repeat the previous recipe, substituting 2 tbs shredded Sichuan pickle for snow pickle, and 100–175 g (4–6 oz) straw mushrooms for the various seaweeds. Serve in a large excavated winter melon, using a quarter of the flesh in the dish.

After stir-frying the various ingredients together as in the previous recipe, and simmering them all in stock for a further 5–6 minutes, pour the contents all into the melon. It is customary in China to place the whole melon in a steamer for 7–8 minutes before serving. For serving, it is best to sit the melon in a large bowl.

Semi-soup Dish of Stir-fried Pickles, Spring Onions and Purée of Beans with Beetroot, Gingko Nuts and Croutons

Serve in a deep-sided dish or in a large bowl. This dish is appealing to rice-eaters mainly because of its rich, creamy savouriness which goes well with plain rice; while the beetroot and croutons provide the variation.
Serves 5–6, with other dishes

3 spring onions
75–100 g (3–4 oz) butter beans
75–100 g (3–4 oz) haricot beans
50 g (2 oz) gingko nuts or lotus
  seeds
75–100 g (3 oz) beetroot
4–5 tbs croutons (or their
  Chinese equivalent: crispy
  rice scrapings)

3 tbs vegetable oil
3 tbs chopped snow pickle
2 slices chopped root-ginger
½ tsp salt
300 ml (½ pint) vegetarian stock
1 vegetarian stock cube
2 tbs butter or margarine
4 tbs top of the milk or cream

Cut spring onion into 5-mm (¼-inch) shavings, separating the white parts from the green. Boil the butter beans and haricot beans for 1 hour. Liquidize them in a blender. Rinse and wash the gingko nuts. Cut beetroot into cubes the size of half a sugar lump. Prepare croutons by frying cubed bread, or dried rice scrapings in hot oil until crisp (these should be freshly prepared before sprinkling over soup).

Heat oil in a saucepan. Add pickles, ginger, salt and the whites of spring onion. Stir them in the hot oil for 1 minute. Add stock, stock cube and gingko nuts. Bring them to boil, and stir them together for 1 minute. Add the purée of beans and butter or margarine. Bring them to a gentle boil. Allow them to simmer gently for 5–6 minutes. Add cubed beetroot and the top of the milk or cream. Stir them into the soup. When the soup reboils, sprinkle its top with crispy croutons or rice scrapings immediately before serving.

Semi-soup Dish of Stir-fried Pickles, Spring Onions and Green Peas with Butter Beans

Although this is a simple dish to cook, it is appealing to the rice-eater for the same reason as the previous recipe. It should be served in a deep-sided dish or a large bowl for the diners to scoop or spoon on to the rice in their rice bowls. Since the food materials and ingredients in most Chinese stir-fried dishes are cut into strips, slices, diced cubes or left in chunky pieces, these rich, creamy, porridgy dishes which can be spooned on to the rice are a welcome change from normal dishes.

Serves 5–6, with other dishes

3 tbs snow pickle

3 spring onions

225 g (8 oz) butter beans

3 tbs vegetable oil

100 g (4 oz) fresh or frozen green peas

1 tsp salt

300 ml (½ pint) vegetarian stock

1 vegetarian stock cube

4 tbs top of the milk

1½ tbs butter or margarine

Coarsely chop pickles. Cut spring onions into 3-mm (⅛-inch) shavings (separating whites from the greens). Soak beans for 3–4 hours. Boil in water for 1 hour, and liquidize in a blender.

Heat oil in a saucepan or casserole. When hot, add the white of the spring onions and pickles. Stir them over medium heat for 1 minute. Add the peas and salt and stir the ingredients together for 1½ minutes. Pour in the stock, and add the crumbled stock cube. When the latter has dissolved and the contents start to boil, add the liquidized beans. Bring contents to a gentle boil, stirring all the time. Simmer and stir for 3 minutes. Add milk and butter or margarine. When it has melted, sprinkle with the greens of the spring onion.

Steaming

Steaming as a method of cooking is much more widely used in China than in the West. There is always a big pan or cauldron of boiling water in a Chinese kitchen due to the vast amount of rice which is cooked daily, and the steam generated can be used to cook other foods. You will seldom see an oven in a Chinese kitchen, which means that very few dishes are roasted, while innumerable dishes are steamed. However, because of the high water content of most vegetables, where the aim during the process of cooking is more to reduce the water content and therefore to concentrate the flavour, rather than to increase it through a process of wet-cooking (i.e. boiling or steaming), steaming is not a method widely adopted for cooking vegetables. It is used much more as part of another process: for example, marinating and steaming, stir-frying and steaming, steaming and dousing with blazing oil. Using hot oil in the process of steaming is an essential part of the Chinese cookery concept, since it is the Chinese theory that flavours are released and concentrated only if food materials are subjected – even though very shortly – to the high temperature of hot oil. The following few recipes illustrate how steaming is used in conjunction with stir-frying and the treatment of hot oil.

Steamed Marrow with Shredded Mushrooms
Serves 5–6

1 medium-sized marrow (about 1.5 kg/3½ lb)
4 medium-sized Chinese dried mushrooms
2–3 dried red chillies
450 ml (¾ pint) vegetarian stock
2 slices root-ginger, finely shredded
1 tsp salt
pepper to taste
1 vegetarian stock cube
4 tbs vegetable oil
2 tbs soya sauce

Clean and scrape the marrow (to remove tough outer skin). Cut the marrow into oblong pieces measuring 7.5 × 4 cm (3 × 1½ inches). Soak the mushrooms in boiling water for half an hour, remove stems and cut caps into shreds. Chop chillies, discarding pips and stems.

Place the marrow pieces in a large, deep-sided, heatproof dish or Pyrex glass bowl. Add stock, sprinkle with shredded ginger, salt and pepper and the crumbled stock cube. Insert glass bowl or heatproof dish with contents into steamer and steam for half an hour. Turn the contents over and steam for a further 15 minutes.

Meanwhile, heat the oil in a small pan or wok. When very hot, add shredded chilli and mushrooms. Stir them in the oil for 2–2½ minutes (the contents should be boiling). Remove the bowl or dish of marrows from the steamer (pour away any excess liquid). Pour the chilli-oil and mushrooms evenly over the marrows. Sprinkle them with soya sauce and serve. Take the dish or bowl of marrows to the dining table for the diners to help themselves from.

Steamed and Stir-fried Carrots and Turnips
Serves 5–6

450g (1lb) large carrots	3tbs vegetable oil
450g (1lb) white turnips	2tbs yellow bean sauce
3 slices root-ginger	1tbs soya sauce
150ml (¼ pint) vegetarian stock	1tbs hoisin sauce
½tsp salt	2tbs red wine
a pinch pepper	2tsp sugar
2 spring onions	1½tbs butter
2 cloves garlic	

Scrape clean the carrots and turnips, and cut them slantwise into triangular pieces measuring approximately 6 × 5cm (2½ × 2 inches). Shred the ginger. Place the vegetables and ginger in a heatproof dish. Add the stock, salt and pepper. Insert the contents into a steamer, and steam for half an hour.

Meanwhile, cut the spring onions into 6-mm (¼-inch) shavings and coarsely chop the garlic. Heat oil in a large frying pan. When hot, add the spring onion, garlic, yellow bean sauce, soya sauce, hoisin sauce, red wine and sugar, and stir them together for 1 minute. Drain the carrots and turnips of any excess liquid. Pour the vegetables into the frying pan, add butter, and stir-fry them with the sauce ingredients in the pan over high heat for 2 minutes. Stir and turn until every piece of vegetable is well coated with sauce. Serve on a well-heated deep-sided dish for the diners to consume with rice.

Steamed Asparagus with Egg Sauce
Serves 4–5

700–900g (1½–2lb) (1 large bundle) fresh asparagus	150ml (¼ pint) vegetarian stock
Egg Sauce:	½ vegetarian stock cube
1 spring onion	1tbs cornflour blended in 3tbs water
2 Chinese salt eggs	3tbs butter
2 fresh eggs	pepper to taste
1½tbs vegetable oil	2tbs dry sherry

Clean the asparagus thoroughly, and remove the tougher end of the stems. Place the asparagus in a colander, and insert them into a steamer. Steam vigorously for 25–30 minutes.

Coarsely chop spring onion and salt eggs. Beat eggs lightly in a cup or bowl. Heat oil in a small saucepan or wok. When hot, add the spring onion and salt eggs. Stir them together for 1 minute over medium heat. Add stock and crumbled stock cube. Stir until contents boil. Add blended cornflour, stir until contents thicken. Remove pan or wok from heat. After quarter of a minute, stir in the beaten egg, butter, pepper and sherry. Continue to stir until mixture is consistent. Place the hot, freshly steamed asparagus on a well-heated serving dish. Pour the sauce over them and serve.

Steamed Courgettes in Mushroom Sauce
Serves 4–5

4–5 medium-sized courgettes (about 700g/1½lb)	1½tbs butter
300ml (½ pint) mushroom sauce (page 107)	

Clean and cut courgettes slantwise into 4-cm (1½-inch) sections. Place them in a steamer and steam vigorously for 5–6 minutes.

Heat mushroom sauce and butter in a saucepan or wok. When boiling, add the steamed courgettes. Stir and turn them for 2–3 minutes. Transfer them to a well-heated serving dish, and serve.

Steamed Cauliflower in Black Bean and Tomato Sauce
Serves 4–5

1 large cauliflower	150ml (¼ pint) black bean and
1½tbs butter	tomato sauce (page 108)

Cut cauliflower vertically into quarters, after removing most of the green leaves and the tougher parts of the stem. Place the four pieces of cauliflower in a colander, insert them in a steamer, and steam vigorously for 18 minutes.

Heat butter and sauce in a small saucepan or wok, stirring it a few times, until it boils.

Transfer the cauliflower on to a well-heated serving dish, pour the boiling sauce over them and serve.

4 Rice

Rice is the central point of all Chinese meals. Other dishes served, which may range from two to three on the table, to seven or eight, are all there to accompany and complement rice, be they meat, poultry, fish, seafood, vegetables or soup. A vegetable buffet of a dozen items may be served on the table to include a whole fish, a large fowl, knuckle of pork or a leg of lamb, a selection of soups and stir-fried dishes, yet the meal is quite incomplete unless there is ample rice to complement them. The only time when rice is not served is at a formal banquet, when the dishes are served as courses, one after another, interspersed with wine drinking and toasting. As there are often a dozen courses or more, the Chinese banquet tends to become very lengthy and over-rich.

But the majority of people are much happier when there is ample rice to accompany their savoury dishes, and they much prefer to sit down to a good family dinner, or an informal dinner party, where rice is served to complement all the dishes served. After all, we are rice-eaters, we need rice to cushion off the richness or spiciness of savoury dishes. We enjoy the sensation of tucking in to the rice to the accompaniment of a variety of savoury food and sauces, and washing and watering them down with savoury soup. Drinking and washing down rice and savoury foods with soup is a sensation peculiar to the enjoyment of eating Chinese food. We Chinese do not drink water at mealtimes – least of all iced water! – nor do we absolutely require tea or wine, although we would sip at them if they are there, for there is always the provision of one or more soups, which are drunk continually throughout the meal. It is probably the diluting effect of soups, and the ample amount of vegetables consumed, some in the soups themselves, which make most Chinese foods so easily digestible and comparatively healthy. Rice and vegetables are indeed the staple diet of the Chinese. Meat, fish and seafood, like spices, are consumed only in small quantities as accompaniments to rice. In China when you ask a person whether he or she has eaten, you would say, 'Have you had rice?'

Rice is cooked in two main ways in China: plain boiled or steamed. Both these should be dry and flaky, and are normally served at lunch and dinner. But at breakfast in China rice is usually eaten in the soft, porridgy form called soft rice, or congee (*Chou* in Chinese).

These two basic rices can be further extended into numerous variations, such as a variety of fried rice, vegetable rice, topped rice and savoury soft rice (or congee) to suit people's palates, and the time of the day.

Soft porridgy rice with no other added ingredients may seem oversimple, bland, and even insipid, but to connoisseurs it can be one of the most welcoming foods devised by man. Eaten at breakfast, it is very warming, cleansing and refreshing, and to the invalid or semi-invalid it can be one of the most comforting and easily digestible of all foods. It is a pleasure to eat when accompanied by only a very small amount of pickles, salted or preserved eggs, or a few drops of good quality soya sauce. Eating congee with these uncomplicated accompaniments while lying in bed is almost a part of the Chinese racial childhood memory!

Although cooking rice is simple, it should be done with great care.

Plain Boiled Rice

It is easier to measure rice by volume than by weight. For ordinary *long-grain* rice the quantities are:

1 cup or small bowl of rice to 1¾ cup or bowl of water (enough for two)

2 cups or bowls of rice to 3 cups or bowls of water

3 cups or bowls of rice to 4¼ cups or bowls of water

With *oval-grain* rice, the percentage of water can be slightly reduced by a quarter cup or bowl, per cup or bowl of rice to be cooked.

Rinse and drain the rice a couple of times. Add it to a heavy saucepan or casserole with a fitting lid. Pour in the correct amount of water. Place the pan or casserole over medium heat, and bring the contents to boil. Boil for 3 minutes. Cover firmly, and leave contents to simmer over the lowest heat for 10 minutes. Turn the heat off altogether. Do not open the lid, but allow the rice to stand and continue to cook in the remaining heat for a further 10 minutes. By that time the rice should be ready to serve. Fluff it up with a wet spoon or chopsticks.

Cooked rice should keep warm easily for half an hour if not removed from the cooker or placed in a draughty spot. If it does become cool it can easily be heated up by pouring in a few tablespoons of boiling water, turning on the heat underneath the pan for 1–2 minutes, and stirring.

Steamed Rice

Steaming is partly 'wet-cooking', and food materials do not dry up as readily as when cooked or heated over a naked flame, so approximately 20 per cent less water is used than for boiled rice. Therefore, to steam 1 cup rice you add 1¼ cups water; for 2 cups rice you add 2½ cups water; and 3 cups rice you add 4 cups water.

Rinse and drain the rice. Put the washed rice into a large or deep heatproof bowl or basin. Add the correct amount water, and leave the rice to soak for half an hour.

Place the bowl containing the rice on a rack in a large pan containing 5–7.5 cm (2–3 inches) water: the water surface should not reach higher than 10 cm (4 inches) below the rim of the bowl. Cover the bowl and bring the water to boil.

Continue to simmer over gentle heat for 30 minutes, when the rice should be ready. Fluff the rice with a wet spoon or chopsticks, and serve by bringing the bowl to the table, which should help to keep the rice hot.

Not infrequently in China rice is steamed in individual bowls, and then brought to the table and served to each diner in the very bowl in which it has been cooked. In the winter the numerous steaming bowls of rice on the dining table present a very appealing and welcoming sight.

Baked Rice

In a modern Western kitchen rice can be baked very conveniently in an oven; if only to get it out of the way during cooking, when many other dishes need to be on the cooker. It is probably best to use a casserole with a heavy lid, and the proportion of water used to cook with the rice should be in the same ratio as for boiled rice (page 92).

Rinse and drain the rice. Put rice and water in the correct proportion into a casserole. Bring contents to boil on the cooker for 2–3 minutes. Cover the casserole, and insert into a preheated oven at 400°F/200°C, gas mark 6, to bake for 12 minutes. Reduce heat to 350°F/180°C, gas mark 4, and continue to bake at this lower temperature for 12 minutes. Then the rice should be ready to serve. Fluff the rice with a wet spoon or a pair of wet chopsticks, and bring the casserole to the table, for the diners to serve themselves.

Brown Rice

Brown rice is becoming increasingly more popular because of the digestive value of the bran, and for its nutrients. Brown rice should be cooked in largely the same manner as ordinary white rice in the previous three recipes. The only difference is that nearly half as much water again is needed for the cooking, which should be continued at low heat for twice the length of time.

Rice cooked in these ways can be used for various forms of fried rice, vegetable rice, or served as a dish of topped rice, an economic and self-contained meal for one. Nowadays this is becoming a more and more popular way of eating in China, as people have become more mobile and can't count upon eating in large family or work groups any more.

Fried Rice

Almost any food material which can be chopped small can be used for making fried rice. One of the simplest and yet most popular fried rice dishes is egg fried rice.

Egg Fried Rice

Simple as it is, this is a satisfying dish to eat even with only a very limited amount of accompaniments, such as some chopped pickles, or just a tablespoon or two of soya sauce.

Serves 2–3, with at least one other savoury dish

1 medium-sized onion	2 spring onions
2 eggs	3½ tbs vegetable oil
1 tsp salt	1½ bowls cold cooked rice

Slice and coarsely chop onion. Break eggs into a cup, add salt, and beat with a fork for 10 seconds. Clean and cut spring onions into fine shavings.

Heat oil in a frying pan or wok. When hot, add chopped onions and stir-fry in the hot oil for 45 seconds. Pour the salted beaten egg into one side of the pan or wok, and add the rice on the other side. When the eggs are about to set, scramble them, then bring them over and mix evenly with the rice which is being stir-fried in the same pan. Sprinkle the contents with half the spring onion shavings. Turn and stir the ingredients together.

Serve by transferring the contents into a large serving bowl or into individual bowls, and sprinkle the top of the fried rice with the remainder of the spring onion shavings.

Vegetable Fried Rice
Almost any kind of vegetable can be chopped, stir-fried and mixed into the fried rice. Favourite ingredients are mushrooms and chopped pickles. Fried rice cooked with multi-ingredients can be eaten with satisfaction even without other accompaniments. It is most suitable to prepare when there is a lot of leftover food lying about. Serve in a large common serving bowl, or in 3–4 individual bowls. Sprinkle the contents in the bowls with chopped spring onions, and 1½ tbs soya sauce.
Serves 2–3, or serve with 1–2 other dishes

1 medium-sized onion	1½ tsp salt
1 medium-sized young carrot	5 tbs vegetable oil
1 medium-sized pepper	3–4 tbs green peas
2 medium-sized tomatoes	75 g (3 oz) bean sprouts
2 spring onions	2 bowls cooked rice
2 eggs	1¼ tbs soya sauce

Cut onion into thin slices. Clean and chop carrot and pepper into 4-mm (⅙-inch) cubes. Cut tomato into 1-cm (½-inch) slices, and further cut into 5-mm (¼-inch) pieces, and spring onions into 4-mm (⅙-inch) shavings. Beat eggs with half the salt.

Heat 4 tbs oil in a large frying pan or wok. When hot, add the onion and carrots. Stir and turn them in the hot oil for 1 minute. Add pepper, peas, bean sprouts, tomato and salt. Stir them all together for one minute, and push all the ingredients to one side of the pan or wok. Add the remaining oil to the other side of the pan. When hot, pour in the beaten egg. Add the rice to the vegetable side of the pan or wok, and spread it evenly over the vegetables. When the eggs are set, scramble them, then bring them over to mix and turn with the vegetables and rice. Continue to stir and turn until the ingredients are evenly mixed. Transfer contents into a large bowl or basin, sprinkle the top with soya sauce and serve.

Vegetable Rice

Vegetable rice differs from fried rice in that it is cooked while the rice is cooking itself. It is possibly less refined than fried rice and very much a dish of the masses. It should really be eaten with at least one other dish.

Vegetable Rice with Aubergine, Carrots, Onions and Green Cabbage

This should be cooked during the preparation of 2–3 cups or bowls of boiled rice or baked rice. One of the attractions of the dish is that much of the flavour and quality of the vegetables will have impregnated themselves into the surrounding rice. Rice and vegetables cooked thus are best served and eaten with at least one stir-fried dish.

Serves 4–5, with at least one other dish

½ medium-sized aubergine	100 g (4 oz) green cabbage
1 medium-sized carrot	3½ tbs vegetable oil
1 medium-sized onion	1 tsp salt

Wash and clean all the vegetables. Cut aubergine into 2.5-cm (1-inch) wedges, roll-cut carrots into sections 1 cm (½ inch) thick, and chop onion and cabbage into thin slices. Heat oil in a frying pan or wok. When hot, add first the carrot and aubergine and stir-fry them over medium heat for 1½ minutes. Add salt, onion and cabbage, and stir and turn the ingredients together for a further 1 minute.

While cooking the boiled rice (when the rice has boiled for 3 minutes, and simmered for 10 minutes) or baked rice (when the rice has boiled for 3 minutes and baked for 10 minutes), most of the moisture will have evaporated. Make a hole in the middle of the rice, into which goes the partially cooked stir-fried ingredients, together with the oil and juices from the pan. Cover the vegetables up with the surrounding rice, and return the saucepan to cook gently for a further 10 minutes, or for the casserole to bake under cover for a further 12 minutes. Without removing the lid, allow the contents to stand and cook in the remaining heat for a further 5 minutes, and the dish should then be ready to serve.

Vegetable Rice with Mushrooms, Onions, Tomatoes and Broccoli
This should be cooked during the preparation of steamed rice. As with the previous recipe for vegetable rice, it is best to eat the dish with a stir-fried savoury dish. A stir-fried dish cooked quickly over high heat has a greater intensity of flavour than a dish which has been cooked largely through steaming, where the flavour has been more lengthily dispersed throughout the whole bulk dish during the process of cooking. It is a matter of balancing a bulk food dish, which is only lightly flavoured, with a dish where the flavour is more concentrated as a result of the way in which it is cooked.
Serves 4–5, with at least one stir-fried dish

1 medium-sized onion	2 cloves garlic
100 g (4 oz) button mushrooms	3½ tbs vegetable oil
2–3 medium-sized tomatoes	1½ tsp salt
100 g (4 oz) broccoli	

Cut onion into thin slices. Cut each mushroom into halves or quarters, and the tomatoes into quarters and each segment into halves. Cut or break broccoli into florets or ½-inch sliced pieces. Crush and chop garlic.

Heat oil in a frying pan or wok. When hot, add onion, broccoli and garlic. Stir-fry over medium heat for 1½ minutes. Add mushrooms and salt, and stir-fry for another minute. Add the tomato and continue stir-frying for 1 more minute.

While in the process of cooking steamed rice, and after the rice has been steamed for 20 minutes, make a hole in the middle and transfer the contents of the frying pan into the hole in the rice. Cover it up with the surrounding rice and return the basin to steam under cover for a further 12 minutes, and the vegetable rice should then be ready to serve.

Soft Rice or Congee

Porridgy soft rice is a Chinese institution, a taste for which can only be acquired through having it for breakfast for some seasons. Its appeal and character lie in its being warm, comforting and refreshing, and these qualities are enhanced when quantities of the rice are eaten with small amounts of strong-tasting, spicy, salted, smoked, pickled, preserved and sometimes aromatic foods (such as roasted salted peanuts). What is attractive about soft rice is emphatically not its savouriness or tastiness, but its total lack of either; perhaps it is this invariability (like porridge) which makes it feel as if it is one of the cornerstones of life. It therefore deserves to be cooked with care.

Plain Soft Rice or Congee

The hot pot or pan of soft rice is often brought to the table, or placed on a side table, for people to help themselves at breakfast time. Soft rice is also served for midnight suppers (after lengthy mahjong games, for example). Because of the high heat content of congee, cold leftover savoury dishes are often brought out from the pantry and served with hot congee without needing to be reheated.

Serves 5–6, with a small amount of highly seasoned foods

175–200 g (6–7 oz) long-grain rice	75–100 g (3–4 oz) glutinous rice
175–200 g (6–7 oz) oval-grain rice	2.25–2.75 litres (4–5 pints) water

Rinse, wash and drain the rice a couple of times. Add it to a large deep saucepan with the water. Bring contents to boil, stir and simmer over gentle heat for 30 minutes. Partially cover and reduce heat to very low. Continue to simmer slowly for 1½ hours, stirring now and then. At the end of that time the rice will have absorbed all the water, and become a white, consistent gruel. It will keep hot or warm for a long time, but even if it is allowed to get cool or cold, it can be readily reheated. Unlike Scots porridge, a supply of it for breakfast can be cooked for two or more days.

Savoury Vegetable Soft Rice or Savoury Congee

In contrast to plain soft rice or congee, savoury congee has unlimited variations. In non-vegetarian cooking there are such famous savoury congees as sampan congee (with seafood), the Cantonese chicken congee, or the Nanking pressed duck congee, and so on. Even in vegetarian cooking, where the number of ingredients used is necessarily limited, the range is considerable. The aim is to produce a soft rice which is only mildly but generally savoury. Whichever vegetables are cooked in it, the length of cooking time allows the flavour to blend into the rice. But its appeal is highlighted by the small bits of highly seasoned foods (such as salted, pickled and marinated foods) which are dispersed and embedded in the soft rice. These will only have been cooked for a short time and the flavours will not yet have spread to the rice. The same effect is produced when a large dollop or two of highly seasoned or savoury sauces (see pages 106–10) are spilled on top of the soft rice just before serving. The same sauces are equally good with flaky, plain boiled rice served as topped rice; that is, without the usual accompaniment of several savoury dishes.

Savoury Vegetable Soft Rice with Cabbage, Pickle and Bean Sprouts
Serve hot, and leave people to help themselves from the cooking pot. As savoury soft rice is an informal snack, no formality should be observed in its eating and serving. Most people are expected to help themselves to more than one helping.
Serves 4–5

350 g (12 oz) heart of Chinese or savoy cabbage	1½ vegetarian stock cubes
3 tbs vegetable oil	75–100 g (3–4 oz) bean sprouts
1 tsp salt	2½ tbs chopped snow pickle
1.2–1.5 litres (2–2½ pints) cooked soft rice	

Wash and cut cabbage heart into 5 × 2.5 × 4-cm (2 × 1 × 1½-inch) pieces. Heat oil in a large heavy saucepan. When hot, add salt and cabbage, and stir-fry them together for 2 minutes. Pour in the soft rice, and add crumbled stock cube and 150 ml (¼ pint) water. Stir them together so that the ingredients are evenly distributed. Continue to cook and simmer gently over very low heat for 1 hour, until the cabbage has become so soft that it almost becomes part of the rice. Sprinkle the contents with bean sprouts and chopped pickle. Stir a few times, cook for a further 4–5 minutes and serve.

Savoury Vegetable Soft Rice with Broccoli (or Asparagus) Stems, Carrots, Pickle and Salted Duck Eggs
Serves 4–5

350g (12oz) broccoli (or asparagus) stems	1 tsp salt
2 medium-sized carrots	1½ vegetarian stock cubes
2–3 salted duck eggs (page 49)	1.2–1.5 litres (2–2½ pints) cooked soft rice
2 spring onions	1½ tbs chopped snow pickle
3 tbs vegetable oil	

Cut the broccoli or asparagus stems into 4 × 1-cm (1½ × ½-inch) pieces. Clean and cut carrots slantwise into 1-cm (½-inch) slices. Chop duck eggs into 5-mm (¼-inch) pieces. Cut spring onions into 1-cm (¼-inch) shavings (separating the white parts from the green).

Heat oil in a heavy saucepan or casserole. When hot, add broccoli, carrots and salt, and stir-fry them together for 2 minutes. Add 150 ml (¼ pint) water and crumbled stock cube, and pour in the soft rice. Stir them together until the ingredients are evenly distributed. Continue to cook and simmer gently over very low heat for 1 hour, until the vegetables are well cooked and have almost become part of the soft rice. Add half the chopped salted eggs, and the whites of the spring onion. Stir them together a few times, and cook gently for a further 4–5 minutes. Sprinkle the top of the soft rice with the remainder of the chopped duck eggs and the greens of the spring onions. Serve hot, as above.

Savoury Vegetable Soft Rice with Dried and Fresh Mushrooms, Salted Kelp, Braised Bamboo Shoots, Chopped Watercress and Soya-braised Eggs
Serves 4–5

5–6 medium-sized Chinese dried mushrooms	75–100g (3–4oz) braised bamboo shoots (available canned)
225g (8oz) fresh button mushrooms	75–100g (3–4oz) kelp

3 soya-braised eggs	1½ vegetarian stock cubes
3–4 tbs watercress	1.2–1.5 litres (2–2½ pints)
3 tbs vegetable oil	cooked soft rice
½ tsp salt	

Soak dried mushrooms in 150 ml (¼ pint) boiling water for half an hour (retaining the water), and cut each cap into quarters. Cut each button mushroom into 1-cm (½-inch) slices, and cut braised bamboo shoots into 4-cm (1½-inch) sections. Wash kelp and cut into similar-sized pieces. Cut soya eggs into 5-mm (¼-inch) pieces. Coarsely chop watercress.

Heat oil in a large saucepan or casserole. When hot, add dried mushrooms, kelp and braised bamboo shoots. Stir-fry them together for 2 minutes. Add fresh mushrooms and salt, and continue to stir-fry the ingredients together for 2 minutes. Pour in the mushroom water and stock cube and the soft rice. Stir and turn the contents together so that they are evenly distributed. Continue to cook and simmer gently for 1 hour, until the vegetables have softened and almost become part of the soft rice. Sprinkle the contents with half the chopped watercress and soya eggs. Stir a few times, and continue to cook gently for a further 4–5 minutes.

Sprinkle the top of the soft rice with the remainder of the chopped watercress and soya eggs just before serving. Serve hot, as above.

Topped Rice or Cooked Rice with Savoury Toppings

Topped rice reflects the changing scene of Chinese eating. In the past, and even on the majority of occasions today, a Chinese meal is a communal affair, where people dine together (be they family, friends or workmates) and the dishes are shared by all those at the table. It is rather like having a sit-down hot buffet, where each diner brings only his or her bowl of rice, and partakes of all the savoury dishes served on the table. The Chinese, whether abroad or at home, have become more and more mobile, so they find themselves dining on their own much more frequently. On these occasions he or she will have their meals served to them in individual portions rather than from dishes served in large buffet spreads, where the diners can simply help themselves.

To meet the requirements of the average Chinese, the best way to serve an essentially Chinese meal in individual portions is to have rice served as a bed in a large bowl or a deep-sided dish, and to have it topped with a miniature dish or two (a case of Chinese *cuisine minceur*!), where preferably at least one dish should have a sauce (to provide the 'gravy') – and if there are two dishes served they should, if possible, be prepared from contrasting ingredients – and the other should be crunchy. And in the combination, if one dish is rich and spicy, the other should have a lighter, fresher and more natural flavour. On the other hand, one might be limited to serving just one dish for an individual portion. In such instances one should choose a dish which combines both the rich and spicy foods, as well as the lighter, fresher and more natural-tasting ones.

Luckily, there are scores of Chinese dishes which are qualified to fulfil these guidelines. If you scan the dishes contained in the section of stir-fried vegetable dishes (pages 62–80), you will notice that there are at least a dozen dishes which are appropriate. If they do not entirely fulfil these requirements, I recommend that you use the foods from two different dishes as garnish or full-portion toppings on rice so that you have several portions of composite topped-rice dishes (or meals): say, for example, a simple, light-tasting dish of Stir-fried Young Cabbage with Root-ginger and Snow Pickles (page 66) with the much spicier Sichuan Hot-braised Stir-fried Aubergine (page 77); or the comparatively dry Four Soya-braised Chunky Vegetables (page 76) can be used in conjunction with the soupy dish of Stir-fried Semi-soup Dish of Mushrooms, Pickles, Braised Bamboo Shoots, Broccoli, Transparent Noodles and Seaweed (page 83).

The appeal of these miniature, topped-rice, 'self-contained' meals is readily enhanced by Chinese homemade pickles, soya-marinated and salted vegetables and savoury vegetable sauces, although these are only used in small quantities.

Homemade Pickles

These are generally made from any three, four or five of the following vegetables:

cucumber, carrot   celery, onion
radish, turnip   leeks, green beans
white cabbage (Chinese or   green pepper, red pepper
  savoy)   spring onion, root-ginger

Pickles are usually made in thoroughly cleaned, airtight jars (glazed earthen, or glass), and for 1–1½ quarts you will need 1.75–2.25 litres (3–4 pints) cold boiled water, 1¼ tbs salt, 3–4 chilli peppers, 2 tsp Sichuan peppercorns (lightly pounded), 1½ tbs sugar, 5–6 slices root-ginger, 2 tbs white rum, gin or vodka. The vegetables should be thoroughly cleaned, trimmed and peeled (if preferred), then well drained and cut into large pieces.

Pour the cold boiled water into the jar. First add the salt, chillies, peppercorns, ginger, spirit and sugar, followed by the selected vegetables. Firmly screw or press on the top of the jar and see that it is airtight. Place the jar in a cool place, and let it stand for a week before using. The longer the wait, the better the pickles!

The vegetables can be extracted from the jar with a very clean pair of chopsticks, or with tongs, but do not allow any grease to enter the jar. When serving a topped-rice dish, the pickled vegetable may be cut into smaller slices and placed in small quantities of about 1½–2 tbs at the edge of the rice.

Homemade Salted Vegetables

Mustard greens, turnip leaves and collard greens are most generally used. The usual process is to place a heap of vegetables on greaseproof paper and leave for three days, turning and reheaping at the end of each day to allow the vegetables to age and mature.

After three days, cut the vegetables into lengthwise strips, rinse them in cold water, and dry them thoroughly. To ensure that they are thoroughly dried, spread them out to air in a breezy spot for 4–5 hours.

Place the vegetables in a wide-mouth jar in layers 2.5 cm (1 inch) thick, sprinkling the top of each layer with 1½–2 tsp of salt. Repeat this process until you have almost reached the top of the jar. Place a smaller jar inside the wide-mouth jar, and a weight on top of the smaller jar to press down the salting vegetables inside. Leave the vegetables for two days. Turn the vegetables over, and pack them again under pressure for two more days, pouring any accumulated liquid over them. Repeat once more, and after approximately a week's salting the vegetables will be ready for use. They will keep in a refrigerator almost indefinitely.

To use, cut the salted vegetables into 5 mm–1 cm (¼–½-inch) pieces and pile them in small heaps by the edge of the rice to be savoured as a 'side item' along with pickles.

Homemade Soya-marinated Vegetables

Soya-marinated vegetables are yet another form of relish which are consumed extensively in China to augment the variety of flavours to be savoured in a Chinese meal. They can be included even in a miniature meal, such as that of a self-contained dish of topped rice.

The vegetables which are most frequently used are white turnips, carrots, beets, cucumber and green kohlrabi.

Wash the vegetables and dry well. Cut them lengthwise into julienne strips. Place the vegetables in a litre or quart jar, until about three-quarters full, add 1 tsp salt and 1½ tbs sugar. Shake well so that each piece of vegetable is coated. Leave to stand overnight.

Add sufficient good quality soya sauce to just cover the vegetables. As in the case of salted vegetables, use a smaller jar which will slot inside the wide-mouth jar to press down the vegetables, so that all the vegetables are submerged and the air bubbles expelled. After marinating overnight, the soya-marinated vegetables are ready to use as a relish, in the same manner as the salted vegetables and pickles. If preferred, 2–3 tsp of chilli sauce or red chilli oil may be added into the marinade to pep up slightly the spiciness of the relish.

Soya-marinated Shredded Ginger

Since ginger is used extensively in Chinese food and cooking, it is often preserved in shredded form so that it may be produced at a moment's notice. Shredded ginger is also often used as a relish or side item, on a dish of fried rice or topped rice, for those who like its sharp flavour. Since marinated root-ginger contained in a jar keeps for months, it can be made in any quantity to suit your need.

Wash and thoroughly dry the root-ginger. Use a paring knife to scrape off the skin. Wipe and dry each piece with absorbent paper. Use a sharp knife to cut each piece into paper-thin slices, and then further cut into fine shreds, about 2.5–4 cm (1–1½ inches) long. Place them in an airtight jar, and pour in enough light soya sauce to cover (add 1–2 shredded dried chilli peppers if you wish). Leave contents to stand overnight. The shredded ginger is then ready for use.

Savoury Vegetable Sauces

There are a number of savoury vegetable sauces which can be added to rice (whether plain, fried or topped) with beneficial results. They are normally added in quantities of no more than 2–3 tablespoonfuls. On top of the rice, they occupy a place between the larger quantities of topped foods (which make up between a quarter and a third of the actual dish) and the relishes (pickles, salted and marinated vegetables) which are only provided in quantities of a tbs or two. Yet their contribution to a dish of rice can be quite significant. Most of these sauces have a fairly concentrated flavour. Their presence in a topped-rice dish paves the way between the sharp flavour of the relishes, and the more general savoury flavour and quantity of topped foods. When all three of these are present, a dish of topped rice can often be as appealing and satisfying as a complete, multidish Chinese meal.

Savoury Mushroom Sauce

This sauce should be added in quantities of 2–4 tbs to a portion of rice as one of the constituents of a dish of topped rice.
Serves 4–5

225 g (8 oz) mushrooms
6 medium-sized Chinese dried
 mushrooms
2 spring onions
1½ tbs vegetable oil
1½ tbs Sichuan Ja Tsai pickle,
 finely chopped
½ tbs yellow bean sauce
1 tbs soya sauce
½ tbs hoisin sauce
150 ml (¼ pint) vegetarian stock
1 vegetarian stock cube
¼ tsp salt
1½ tbs butter or margarine
1 tsp sesame oil
2½ tsp cornflour blended in
 2 tbs water

Clean and cut mushrooms into thin slices. Soak dried mushrooms in boiling water for half an hour. Remove and discard stems, and cut caps into shreds. Cut spring onion into 6-mm (¼-inch) shavings (separating the whites from the greens).

Heat oil in a saucepan or wok. When hot, add the dried mushrooms, pickles and the whites of spring onions. Stir them in the hot oil for 1½ minutes. Add the mushrooms and continue to stir and turn for 1½ minutes. Add the yellow bean sauce, soya sauce and hoisin sauce and stir them all together for 2 minutes. Pour in the vegetarian stock, add the crumbled vegetarian stock cube, salt and butter or margarine. Cook them together over low heat for 5–6 minutes. Add the greens of the spring onion, butter and sesame oil. Stir and turn them

together for 1 minute. Add the blended cornflour. Stir until
the sauce thickens.

Sichuan Aubergine and Bamboo-shoot Sauce

Use this sauce in the same manner and quantity as in the previous
recipe.
Serves 4–5

1 medium-sized aubergine	200 ml (⅓ pint) vegetarian stock
100 g (4 oz) marinated bamboo shoots (available canned)	1 vegetarian stock cube
	½ tbs light soya sauce
1–2 dried chillies (to taste)	1½ tbs butter or margarine
1–2 fresh chillies (to taste)	1 tsp sesame oil
2 slices root-ginger	2½ tsp cornflour blended in
2½ tbs vegetable oil	2 tbs water
½ tsp salt	

Remove the ends of the aubergine (including the stem), and
cut into pieces the size of quarter of a sugar lump. Cut
marinated bamboo shoots into the same size as the aubergine.
After removing the pips and pulp, finely chop the peppers.
Finely chop the ginger, too.

Heat oil in a saucepan or wok. When hot, add peppers and
ginger, and stir-fry them together for 1 minute. Add the
bamboo shoots, salt and aubergine. Stir and turn them over
high heat with the other ingredients for 2 minutes. Pour in the
stock, add the crumbled stock cube and soya sauce. When
contents boil, stir and cook the ingredients together over low
heat for 10 minutes. Add butter or margarine and sesame oil,
and continue to stir and turn for 1 minute. Add cornflour, stir
until the sauce thickens.

Savoury Tomato and Black-bean Sauce (or Ratatouille Chinoise)

Use and serve in the same manner and quantity as the sauces in the
two previous recipes.
Serves 4–5

5–6 medium-sized tomatoes	1 medium-sized onion
1 tbs salted black beans	4 cloves garlic
2 medium-sized courgettes	3 tbs vegetable oil

½ tsp salt
150 ml (¼ pint) vegetarian stock
2 tsp sugar
3 tbs dry sherry
1 pinch pepper
4 tbs tomato purée
1 vegetarian stock cube

1 tbs light soya sauce
½ tbs dark soya sauce
1½ tbs butter
1 tsp sesame oil
2½ tsp cornflour blended in
   2 tbs water

Cut tomato into sugar-lump-sized pieces, soak black beans for 5 minutes, drain and mash. After removing their stems, cut courgettes into half the size of the tomato pieces. Cut onion into very thin slices. Crush and coarsely chop garlic.

Heat oil in a saucepan or wok. When hot, add the onion and stir in the hot oil for 1 minute. Add garlic, black beans and salt, and continue to stir for half a minute. Add the courgettes and tomatoes, and stir and turn them all together over high heat for 3 minutes.

Add the stock, sugar, sherry, pepper, tomato purée and crumbled stock cube. When contents boil, reduce heat, and cook at a simmer for 7–8 minutes, stirring now and then. Add soya sauce, butter and sesame oil. Stir and cook for 1 more minute. Finally, add blended cornflour. Stir until the sauce thickens.

Egg Sauce with Mashed Butter Beans and Chopped Bean Sprouts
Serve and use in the same manner and quantity as the sauces in the previous recipes.
Serves 4–5

4 eggs
2 spring onions
2 cloves garlic
2 tbs snow pickle
175 g (6 oz) butter beans
3 tbs vegetable oil
200 ml (⅓ pint) vegetarian stock
1 tsp salt

1½ tsp sugar
2 tbs dry sherry
1 vegetarian stock cube
2 tbs butter or margarine
1 tbs light soya sauce
2½ tsp cornflour blended in
   2 tbs water
1 tsp sesame oil

Beat eggs lightly for 10 seconds with a fork. Cut spring onion into 6-mm (¼-inch) shavings (separating the whites from the greens). Coarsely crush garlic and pickle, and mix together with the whites of spring onions. Boil butter beans for 30–45 minutes, or until soft, then drain and mash them.

Heat oil in a saucepan or wok. When hot, add the whites of spring onions, garlic and pickle, and stir them in the hot oil for 1½ minutes. Add the stock and salt, mashed butter beans, sugar, sherry and crumbled stock cube. Stir until the contents are well integrated. When contents boil, reduce to a simmer, and cook gently over low heat for 7–8 minutes. Stir in the beaten eggs. Stir until eggs set and contents have become smooth and consistent. Add butter or margarine and soya sauce, stir and cook for a further half minute. Add cornflour, and stir until the sauce thickens. Sprinkle with sesame oil.

5 Soups

Soup in China is a much more integral part of a meal than in Western cooking. It does not stand alone at the beginning of a meal, to be eaten separately, but is eaten throughout the meal between mouthfuls of other foods. It is meant to complement the other foods rather than to lend more weight to the meal, and in contrast to the other dishes served on the table, which are mostly solids, the average Chinese soups are mostly clear. Large chunks of solid foods, clearly seen suspended in the transparent soup, add flavour to the meal and are picked out with chopsticks to be eaten separately, but the soups themselves are drunk as clear hot drinks to the accompaniment of rice and other solid dishes on the table. However, this does not mean that there are no thick soups in the Chinese repertoire. Indeed many well-known Chinese soups, such as Hot and Sour Soup, Shark's Fin Soup, Westlake Minced Beef Soup, are thick soups, but they are not served very often. Since soups are not meant to lend weight to a meal, it is not customary in Chinese cooking automatically to grind food materials to a pulp and use this as a basic ingredient for porridgy soup, which is the tendency in Western cooking.

We Chinese are very particular about flavour: a soup may be clear but it must be flavoursome. A distinctive flavour can be created from a combination of ingredients, or from using a quantity of one single ingredient, or from the flavour of the original broth. In order to achieve a clear broth, which is usually required to make a Chinese soup, the ordinary vegetarian stock, based on slow-cooked beans (page 30), will need to be strained two or three times. Water is often used instead of stock or broth, since they both require such a considerable time to become absolutely clear. Chunkily cut, hard vegetables are simmered for a period of time and then a small quantity of ingredients such as yeast extract, other vegetable concentrates or seasonings are added to pep up the flavour. Leaf vegetables are normally added only a very few minutes before the soup is ready, to provide both a freshening effect as well as an additional flavour.

Generally in Chinese vegetarian cooking the hard stems or roots of vegetables are cooked in the soup to provide the long-term flavouring, and the leaf vegetables are cooked for just a short time to provide a fresh dimension of flavour, with the seasonings, sauces or flavouring agents only being included to complement the bulk flavour of the dish, and to provide that added zest. Since the main bulk food eaten in a Chinese meal is rice, which is meant to be plain, neutral and bland, it generally requires a tasty soup to complement it.

We shall start with a few simple soups, and the simplest of all is the Egg-Drop Soup.

Egg-Drop Soup

This is often seen on Chinese dinner tables, whether at home, in offices, canteens or student dining rooms. It can be produced in 2–3 minutes. The soup should be served in a large bowl for the diners to help themselves from during the course of the meal.
Serves 4–5

1–2 eggs	750–900 ml (1¼–1½ pints)
2 spring onions	boiling water
1½ tsp salt	300 ml (½ pint) vegetarian stock
pepper to taste	

Beat egg for 10 seconds with a fork or chopsticks. Coarsely chop spring onions (separating the whites from greens).

Add the whites of spring onion, salt and pepper to a saucepan or wok. Pour in the boiling water. When contents have boiled, pour in the beaten eggs very slowly along the prongs of a fork, twirling evenly over the surface of the soup. Sprinkle the spring onion greens into the soup. Add the vegetarian stock and crumbled stock cube. Bring to the boil, stir and serve.

Egg-Drop Soup with Tomatoes
Serves 4–5

Repeat the previous recipe, using 3–4 medium-sized tomatoes. Cut the tomatoes into segments and add them to the soup with the whites of the spring onions. Then proceed in the same manner as in the previous recipe. Adjust the seasonings towards the end as the tomatoes will increase the volume of the soup.

Spinach and Braised Bamboo-shoot Soup
Serve in a large soup bowl for the diners to help themselves from during the meal. Very often a cake of bean curd is cut into sugar-lump-sized cubes and added to the soup for a minute's cooking before serving.
Serves 4–5

450 g (1 lb) fresh spinach	1.2 litres (2 pints) water
100 g (4 oz) braised bamboo shoots (available canned)	1 vegetarian stock cube
3½ tbs vegetable oil	1 tbs light soya sauce
1 tsp salt	1 tbs cornflour blended in 3 tbs water
2 tsp sugar	1 tsp sesame oil

Wash and thoroughly drain spinach. Remove tough stems and discoloured leaves. Cut braised bamboo shoots into 5 cm × 4-mm (2 × ⅙-inch) thin strips.

Heat 2½ tbs oil in a large pan or wok. When hot, add half the spinach. When this has wilted, add the second half with the remaining oil. Sprinkle the spinach evenly with salt and sugar. After 1 minute, remove the spinach and pour away any extracted water.

Heat water in the pan or wok. When it boils, add the bamboo shoots, crumbled stock cube and soya sauce. Allow contents to simmer together for 1½ minutes. Return the spinach into the pan or wok. Stir the contents so that the ingredients are evenly distributed in soup. Adjust the seasonings, then add the blended cornflour. When contents reboil, sprinkle the soup with sesame oil.

Bean Sprout and Soya-bean Soup

Serve in a large soup bowl for the diners to help themselves from during the meal. This is a fairly substantial soup, which should add to the bulk and nourishment of a meal.
Serves 4–5

350 g (12 oz) bean sprouts	600 ml (1 pint) stock
175 g (6 oz) soya beans	½ tsp sugar
1.2 litres (2 pints) water	1 vegetarian stock cube
½ tsp salt	1 tbs light soya sauce
2 spring onions	1 tsp sesame oil
3 tbs vegetable oil	

Wash and shake bean sprouts in water, drain and set aside. Wash, and boil beans in 600 ml (1 pint) of the water with salt. Simmer gently for 1 hour until quite soft. Coarsely chop spring onions.

Heat oil in a large pan or wok. When hot, add the sprouts and stir-fry them together for 2 minutes. Pour the cooked beans and stock into the pan. Add the remaining 600 ml (1 pint) water. When contents reboil, sprinkle the soup with crumbled stock cube and soya sauce. Stir and simmer for 2 minutes. Sprinkle with spring onion and sesame oil and serve.

Cream of Spinach (or Green Cabbage) Soup or Green Jade Soup

This is another fairly substantial soup which should add to the bulk and nourishment of the meal. Its green colour should particularly appeal to the average Western palate, which is used to soups of this type.
Serves 4–5

300g (10oz) young spinach
1 tbs Ja Tsai pickle
1 cake bean curd
2 cloves garlic
3 tbs vegetable oil
1 tsp salt
600 ml (1 pint) water

600 ml (1 pint) vegetarian stock
1 vegetarian stock cube
1½ tbs light soya sauce
1½ tbs butter or margarine
1½ tbs cornflour blended in
  3 tbs water

Clean spinach and remove tough stems and discoloured leaves. Place half the spinach in a blender with half the pickle and reduce to a mince. Repeat with remaining spinach and pickle. Cut bean curd into 6-mm (¼-inch) cubes (or smaller). Coarsely crush and chop garlic.

Heat oil in a saucepan or wok. When hot, add minced spinach, pickle, garlic and salt. Stir-fry over medium heat for 2 minutes. Pour in the water and stir. When contents reboil, add stock and crumbled stock cube. Reboil again and add the chopped bean curd and soya sauce. Allow the contents to simmer together for a further 2 minutes. Adjust the seasonings. Add the butter or margarine and blended cornflour. Turn and stir a few times, and serve.

Cream of Corn Soup with Green Peas, Carrots and Peppers

A very quick and easy soup to make. Yet it is substantial and satisfying.
Serves 4–5

2 tbs vegetable oil
1 tsp salt
50–100g (2–4oz) diced frozen
  peas, carrots and red peppers
175–225g (6–8oz) canned cream
  of corn

600 ml (1 pint) water
300 ml (½ pint) vegetarian stock
1 vegetarian stock cube
1 tbs butter
salt and pepper to taste

Heat oil in a saucepan or wok. When hot, add salt and the frozen vegetables and stir together for half a minute. Pour in the corn and water. When contents come to the boil, add stock and sprinkle with crumbled stock cube and gently simmer for 5–6 minutes. Adjust the seasonings. Stir in the butter and serve.

Chinese White Cabbage Soup

Every winter there seems to be a super-abundant crop of white cabbage in north China. Because of the quantity of the cabbage used to make this soup, it is full of flavour, and is consequently one of the most widely served soups in China for half of the year. It is even served for breakfast sometimes! Although a clear soup, it is often spooned into the diner's rice bowl and the cabbage and rice eaten together with great satisfaction.

Serves 4–5

1 medium-sized Chinese white Tientsin cabbage (1–1.5 kg/2–3 lb)	3 tbs vegetable oil
	1 tsp salt
	1.2 litres (2 pints) water
2 dried red chillies	1 vegetarian stock cube
2 tbs snow pickle	salt and pepper to taste
3–4 Chinese dried mushrooms	

Wash and cut cabbage into 5-cm (2-inch) sections. Cut peppers (remove pips and pulp) and pickles into thin shreds. Soak dried mushrooms in boiling water for half an hour. Remove stems and cut caps into similar thin shreds.

Heat oil in a saucepan or wok. When hot, add salt, pickles, peppers and mushrooms. Stir them together in the hot oil over medium heat for 1½ minutes. Add the cabbage and continue to stir and turn for 2 minutes. Pour in the water and sprinkle contents with crumbled stock cube. When contents reboil, simmer for 10 minutes. Adjust the seasonings, and serve.

White Turnip Soup

There are other Chinese vegetable soups where the quality and character of the soups are derived from the weight and quantity of the vegetable used. They are simple, unfanciful soups with plenty of character. The large quantity of turnips gives the character to this soup. After a comparatively lengthy cooking, the vegetable becomes tender and very appealing when consumed in large chunky pieces, to be eaten with rice and washed down with mouthfuls of soup.

Serves 4–5

700 g (1½ lb) white turnips	2½ tbs vegetable oil
1½ tbs snow pickle	1 tsp salt
1½ tbs Sichuan Ja Tsai pickle	900 ml (1½ pints) water

600 ml (1 pint) double-strained
  vegetarian stock
½ tsp sugar

1 vegetarian stock cube
salt and pepper to taste

Clean and scrape the turnip. Cut it into regular 4×2.5-cm
(1½ × 1-inch) wedges. Coarsely chop pickles. Heat oil in a
saucepan or wok. When hot, add the pickles and stir-fry for 1
minute. Add the turnips, salt and water. Bring contents to
boil. Reduce heat, and allow contents to simmer gently for 40
minutes. Add stock, sugar and crumbled stock cube. Turn
contents over a few times. Adjust the seasonings, cook gently
for 5 more minutes, and serve.

Carrot and Cucumber Soup

Once again, because of the large quantity of carrot and cucumber, the
soup is full of vegetable flavour. For the rice-eater it is an enjoyable
soup to drink and to eat not only because of the richness of the soup
but also because of the vegetables which can be eaten with mouthfuls
of rice.
Serves 4–5

700 g (1½ lb) large young carrots
225 g (8 oz) cucumber
2 spring onions
1½ tbs snow pickle
2½ tbs vegetable oil
4 slices root-ginger

1 tsp salt
900 ml (1½ pints) water
600 ml (1 pint) double-strained
  vegetarian stock
1 vegetarian stock cube
salt and pepper to taste

Scrape and thoroughly clean the carrots. Cut slantwise into
1-cm (½-inch) thick slices. Cut cucumber (including peel) into
2.5-cm (1-inch) wedged pieces, and the spring onions into
4-mm (⅙-inch) shavings (separating whites from greens).
Chop pickles into small pieces.

Heat oil in a saucepan or wok. When hot, add ginger and
pickles, and stir over medium heat for 1 minute. Add carrots,
whites of spring onion, salt and water. Bring contents to boil,
and simmer gently for 35 minutes. Add cucumber, stock and
crumbled stock cube. Continue to cook and simmer for a
further 5–6 minutes. Adjust the seasonings, sprinkle with the
greens of spring onions, and serve.

Marrow (or Winter Melon) Soup with Dried Mushrooms

This is another Chinese soup whose character is determined by the quantity used of a specific vegetable. It is also another satisfying soup to consume with quantities of rice.
Serves 4–5

1 kg (2 lb) marrow	900 ml (1½ pints) water
6–7 medium-sized Chinese dried mushrooms	600 ml (1 pint) double-strained vegetarian stock
2½ tbs vegetable oil	1 vegetarian stock cube
4 slices root-ginger	1½ tbs light soya sauce
1½ tsp salt	salt and pepper to taste

Clean and scrape the marrow thoroughly (removing some of the tougher outer skin). Cut it into 6 × 2.5 × 1-cm (2½ × 1 × ½-inch) pieces. Soak dried mushrooms in boiling water for half an hour. Remove stems, and cut caps into shreds (retaining mushroom water).

Heat oil in a saucepan or wok. When hot, add ginger, salt and mushrooms. Stir-fry them together for 1 minute. Add water, mushroom water and marrow. Bring contents to boil, and simmer gently for 40 minutes. Add stock, crumbled stock cube and soya sauce. Cook and simmer gently for a further 10 minutes. Adjust the seasonings and serve.

Vegetable Stem Soup with Braised Bamboo Shoots and Salted Turnips

The vegetable stems should feel very tender, almost melt in the mouth, yet be redolent with vegetable flavour. Another excellent soup to consume with quantities of rice.
Serves 4–5

225 g (8 oz) broccoli stems	3 slices root-ginger
225 g (8 oz) Chinese cabbage stems	½ tsp salt
half a cauliflower stem	900 ml (1½ pints) water
50 g (2 oz) braised bamboo shoots (available in cans)	600 ml (1 pint) double-strained vegetarian stock
50 g (2 oz) salted turnips (available in cans or jars)	1½ tbs light soya sauce
2½ tbs vegetable oil	1½ vegetarian stock cubes
	salt and pepper to taste

Since the tops and leaves of the vegetables can be used for other purposes, the stems can be cut out and carved into thick double mahjong size pieces. Cut bamboo shoots into thin 2.5-cm (1-inch) strips. Rinse salted turnips in running water and cut into 2.5-cm (1-inch) strips.

Heat oil in a saucepan or wok. When hot, add ginger, bamboo shoots and salted turnips. Stir-fry them together for 1 minute. Add salt, water and all the vegetable stems. Bring contents to boil, and simmer gently for 30 minutes. Add vegetarian stock, soya sauce and crumbled stock cube. Stir and cook gently for a further 5–6 minutes. Adjust the seasonings and serve.

Three Shredded Ingredients and Transparent Noodle Soup

This is considered to be a more refined soup than the previous recipes, in which the vegetables are cut and cooked in chunky pieces, and is often served at dinner parties. The contrast of flavour and texture of the different ingredients all awash in a savoury soup gives the palate a uniquely satisfying sensation.

Serves 4–5

75–100g (3–4oz) Chinese braised bamboo shoots	1 tsp salt
	600 ml (1 pint) water
75–100g (3–4oz) celery	1 vegetarian stock cube
5–6 medium-sized Chinese dried mushrooms	450 ml (¾ pint) double-strained vegetarian stock
50 g (2 oz) transparent bean-starch noodles	1 tbs light soya sauce
	salt and pepper to taste
2 tbs vegetable oil	1 tsp sesame oil
3 slices root-ginger	

Cut bamboo shoots and celery into matchstick shreds. Soak dried mushrooms in boiling water for half an hour. Remove stems, and cut caps into similar shreds (retaining mushroom water). Soak noodles in warm water for 5–6 minutes, and cut into sections 7.5 cm (3 inches) long.

Heat oil in a saucepan or wok. When hot, add ginger and dried mushrooms and stir-fry them together for 1 minute. Add water, salt, crumbled stock cube, noodles, shredded bamboo shoots and celery. Bring contents to boil, and simmer gently for 12 minutes. Add stock, mushroom water and soya sauce, and continue to simmer for a further 3–4 minutes. Adjust the seasonings, sprinkle with sesame oil and serve.

Three Mushroom Soup with Transparent Bean-starch Noodles

This is a refined soup. It should be very savoury and full of mushroom flavour, with the bamboo shoots and noodles providing added interest and contrast in texture.
Serves 4–5

225 g (8 oz) firm button mushrooms
5–6 medium-sized Chinese dried mushrooms
40–50 g (1½–2 oz) ordinary European dried mushrooms (available in packets)
50 g (2 oz) winter bamboo shoots
50 g (2 oz) transparent bean-starch noodles

2 tbs vegetable oil
1 tsp salt
2 slices root-ginger
100–150 g (4–5 oz) Chinese straw mushrooms
450 ml (¾ pint) water
600 ml (1 pint) double-strained vegetarian stock
1 vegetarian stock cube
1 tbs light soya sauce
1 tsp sesame oil

Cut button mushrooms into 6-mm (¼-inch) slices. Soak Chinese dried mushrooms in 150 ml (¼ pint) boiling water for half an hour (retain water). Remove stems and cut caps into quarters. Soak dried mushrooms in 150 ml (¼ pint) boiling water for half an hour (retain water). Cut bamboo shoots into matchstick shreds. Soak noodles in water, drain and cut into 5-cm (2-inch) sections.

Heat oil in a saucepan or wok. When hot, add all the dried mushrooms, salt and ginger. Stir-fry them together for 1½ minutes. Add the button mushrooms, straw mushrooms, bamboo shoots and water. Bring to the boil and simmer gently for 10 minutes. Add noodles, stock, crumbled stock cube, soya sauce and mushroom water. Stir and mix the ingredients together. When contents reboil, simmer them gently together for another 3–4 minutes. Sprinkle with sesame oil, and serve.

Asparagus Soup with 'Needle Mushrooms' and Fried Bean Curd Strips

Apart from its flavour, this soup is interesting in that its main ingredients (asparagus, bean curd and mushrooms) all have such different shapes and textures to intrigue the palate.

Serves 4–5

450–700g (1–1½lb) fresh asparagus
1 cake bean curd
vegetable oil for deep-frying
1½tbs snow pickle
1 small onion
2½tbs vegetable oil
600ml (1 pint) water
1 vegetarian stock cube

100–175g (4–6oz) 'needle mushrooms' (available canned)
1tsp sugar
450ml (¾ pint) double-strained vegetarian stock
1tsp salt
1tbs light soya sauce
2tbs dry sherry

Clean and cut asparagus slantwise into 5-cm (2-inch) sections (removing the tougher roots). Cut bean curd into double sugar-lump-sized rectangular pieces. Deep-fry them for 2½ minutes or until slightly brown. Drain well. Coarsely chop pickles and onion.

Heat oil in a saucepan or wok. Add onion and pickles and stir-fry them over medium heat for 1 minute. Add asparagus and stir-fry with the other ingredients for 2 minutes. Add water, crumbled stock cube, mushrooms and sugar. Bring contents to boil, and simmer gently for 20 minutes. Pour in the stock and bean curd, and add salt, soya sauce and sherry. Continue to simmer for 5 minutes, and serve.

Hot and Sour Soup

This soup has considerable body. A very popular soup in north and central China during the colder months, a bowlful will have a very warming effect in winter anywhere.

Serves 4–5

2½tbs Sichuan Ja Tsai pickle
3 slices root-ginger
1 medium-sized onion
40g (1½oz) tree fungi

5 medium-sized Chinese dried mushrooms
75g (3oz) braised bamboo shoots

25 g (1 oz) bean curd skin
  (optional)
2 spring onions
1½ cakes bean curd
2 eggs
2½ tbs vegetable oil
400 ml (⅔ pint) water
1 tsp salt
5 tbs straw mushrooms
1 pint vegetarian stock
2 vegetarian stock cubes
3–4 tbs green peas

Sauce:
2 tbs cornflour blended in 5 tbs
  water
4 tbs wine vinegar
3 tbs water
1 tbs dry sherry
2 tbs light soya sauce
¼ tsp freshly ground black
  pepper

Cut Ja Tsai pickles and ginger into fine shreds, and the onion into thin slices. Soak and rinse tree fungi, clean well. Soak dried mushrooms in boiling water for half an hour. Remove stems, and cut caps into shreds. Cut bamboo shoots and bean curd skin into matchstick strips and spring onions into 4-mm (⅛-inch) shavings (separate whites from greens). Cut bean curd into sugar-lump-sized cubes. Beat the eggs lightly in a bowl.

Mix the ingredients for the sauce together until consistent. Heat oil in a saucepan or wok. When hot, add ginger, pickle and dried mushrooms. Stir them together over medium heat for 1½ minutes. Add water and salt. When contents come to the boil, add tree fungi, straw mushrooms, bamboo shoots, whites of spring onions, bean curd skin and stock. When contents reboil, reduce heat, and simmer gently for 10 minutes. Stir in the crumbled stock cube, add bean curd, peas and the greens of spring onion. Cook gently for a further 3 minutes. Pour in the sauce mixture slowly and stir, which causes the soup to thicken. Drip beaten egg in a fine stream over the surface of the soup. When it sets, the soup is ready to serve.

6 Noodles

The three main types of Chinese noodles are made of wheat flour, rice flour and bean flour, and they are generally cooked in three different ways: fried noodles or chow mein are stir-fried with other ingredients in a pan or wok; cooked noodles or noodles in gravy are cooked in a pot with sauce or gravy; while soup noodles are cooked and suspended in soup. All noodle dishes are considered to be snacks and are consumed on their own as a small meal at odd times during the day. They can also be added to the several dishes served during a meal to augment the meal; or they can be served as a soup to start or, more usually, to finish a meal. Wheat-flour noodles are the common noodles of the north where the climate is too dry for growing rice; in the south and along the Yangtze valley, where rice is abundantly grown, half the noodles consumed are made of rice flour. Bean-flour noodles are a special category which are very white in colour, but become almost transparent when cooked. Unlike other noodles, prepared and eaten as bulk food, they are cooked as a savoury dish, served with several other savoury dishes on the table and eaten with rice. They are very rarely served as a snack entirely on their own.

Transparent Bean-starch Noodles

Ants Climbing the Tree (Ma-Yi San Shu)

This is one of the best-known bean-flour noodle dishes – very savoury and aromatic and excellent with rice.

Serves 4–5, with other dishes

150–175 g (5–6 oz) transparent bean-starch noodles	1 tsp salt
	3–4 tbs green peas
5 medium-sized Chinese dried mushrooms	1½ tsp sesame oil
	Sauce:
2 cloves garlic	4 tbs vegetarian stock
2 tbs Sichuan Ja Tsai pickle	¼ tsp salt
75 g (3 oz) braised bamboo shoots (available canned)	1 tbs light soya sauce
	½ vegetarian stock cube
4–5 tbs roasted peanuts	1 tbs wine vinegar
2 spring onions	1½ tbs dry sherry
4½ tbs vegetable oil	

Soak bean-starch noodles in boiling water for 6–7 minutes, drain, and cut with scissors into sections 7.5–10 cm (3–4 inches) long. Soak dried mushrooms in boiling water for half an hour. Drain, remove stems, and cut caps into coarse grains. Crush garlic and coarsely chop pickles and bamboo shoots. Crush and pound roasted peanuts. Cut spring onions into fine shavings (separating the whites from greens). Mix the sauce ingredients together until blended.

Heat 4 tbs oil in a large frying pan or wok. When hot, add the chopped pickles, garlic, salt, bamboo shoots, dried mushrooms and whites of spring onion and stir-fry them over medium heat for 2 minutes. Add the noodles and turn and mix them with the other ingredients for 2 minutes until they are well mixed. Pour the sauce evenly over the contents, and continue to stir, mix and turn over medium heat for a further 2 minutes. Remove the contents, and transfer them to a serving dish. Add remaining oil into the pan or wok. When hot, add first the crushed peanuts and stir in the hot oil for half a minute, followed by the peas and greens of the spring onions. Stir them all together for a further half a minute. Sprinkle these and the sesame oil evenly over the noodles in the dish.

Cooked Transparent Bean-starch Noodles with Fresh Vegetables
This dish is full of vegetable qualities which are enhanced by the contrasting character of the very savoury noodles. It can be eaten on its own, but the Chinese are more likely to have it as an accompaniment to rice.
Serves 4–5, with other dishes

150–175 g (5–6 oz) transparent bean-starch noodles
2 cloves garlic
3 slices root-ginger
2 spring onions
75–100 g (3–4 oz) French beans
75–100 g (3–4 oz) broccoli tops
75–100 g (3–4 oz) asparagus spears

75–100 g (3–4 oz) bean sprouts
3 tbs vegetable oil
1 tsp salt
300 ml (½ pint) double-strained vegetarian stock
1 vegetarian stock cube
4 tbs white wine
1½ tbs light soya sauce
1 tsp sesame oil

Soak noodles in hot water for 7–8 minutes. Drain and cut with scissors into sections 7.5–10 cm (3–4 inches) long. Coarsely crush and chop garlic. Shred ginger, and cut spring onions into 4-mm (⅙-inch) shavings (separating the white parts from the green). Top and tail the beans, trim the broccoli and asparagus into regular-sized pieces.

Heat oil in a large saucepan or wok. When hot, add ginger, garlic, whites of spring onion and salt. Stir-fry them together over medium heat for 1½ minutes. Add all the other vegetables. Stir and turn them with the other ingredients for the next 3 minutes. Add the stock, and sprinkle contents with crumbled stock cube. When contents boil, allow them to simmer gently for 3 minutes. Add the noodles, which will soak up all the liquid in the pan or wok. Reduce heat and simmer slowly for a further 4–5 minutes, stirring and turning now and then. Sprinkle contents with wine, soya sauce and sesame oil. Stir, turn once more, and serve.

Transparent Bean-starch Noodles with Egg Sauce
This is one of the very few occasions when bean-starch noodles are served on their own, rather than being eaten with rice.

Serves 4–5, with 1–2 other dishes

100–150g (4–5oz) bean-starch noodles
2 slices root-ginger
3 spring onions
4 eggs
2½tbs vegetable oil
½tsp salt

600ml (1 pint) vegetarian stock
1½tbs butter or margarine
Sauce:
2tbs light soya sauce
3tbs dry sherry
1tbs red bean curd 'cheese'
3tbs vegetarian stock

Soak noodles in boiling water for 7–8 minutes. Drain and cut with scissors into sections 7.5–10cm (3–4 inches) long. Cut ginger into fine shreds, and spring onions into 1-cm (½-inch) sections. Beat eggs lightly with fork or chopsticks for 10–12 seconds. Mix sauce ingredients together until consistent.

Heat oil in a saucepan or wok. When hot, add ginger, salt, and whites of spring onions. Stir them together for half a minute. Add half the beaten eggs. Stir until the eggs set. Pour in the stock and the sauce mixture. Stir until the contents boil. Add butter or margarine, and the remainder of the beaten egg. Stir quickly and remove from heat before eggs are completely set. Sprinkle contents with the greens of the spring onion.

Divide the noodles into 4–5 bowls. Pour an appropriate amount of sauce over the contents of each bowl of noodles.

'Buddhist Delight' (Lo-Han Jai)

This is one of the most popular vegetarian dishes, which is served in Chinese temples and monasteries. There are always hundreds of enshrined minor gods, called 'Lo-Hans', who presumably have to be fed. The dish is prepared by stewing together a good range of dried vegetables with a range of fresh vegetables, together with bean-starch noodles, cooked in a sauce made from stock and seasoned with a few flavouring agents.

As this is a very large dish with lots of ingredients, it will have to be served in a very large serving bowl. This is placed at the centre of the table for diners to help themselves from with both chopsticks and a serving spoon.

Serves 8–10

Dried ingredients:
6 medium-sized Chinese dried
  mushrooms
3 tbs 'tree-ear' fungi
3 tbs 'hair seaweed'
50 g (2 oz) dried bamboo shoots
75 g (3 oz) dried chestnuts
3 lily bud stems
2 dried bean curd sticks
4 slices lotus roots or gingko
  nuts
3–4 tbs lotus nuts
100–150 g (4–5 oz) bean-starch
  noodles
1 tsp salt
3 tbs vegetable oil
Fresh ingredients:
1 stick celery, shredded
1 medium-sized sweet pepper,
  shredded
50 g (2 oz) fresh mushrooms,
  shredded

2 spring onions, cut into 2.5-
  cm/1-inch sections
50–75 g (2–3 oz) bean sprouts,
  blanched
50–75 g (2–3 oz) Chinese white
  cabbage, shredded
50–75 g (2–3 oz) cauliflower,
  broken into small florets
50–75 g (2–3 oz) broccoli, broken
  into small florets
2½ tbs vegetable oil
½ tsp salt
2 tsp sesame oil
Stock and sauce:
600 ml (1 pint) vegetarian stock
2½ tbs light soya sauce
¼ tsp salt
1 tbs bean curd 'cheese'
1½ tbs rice wine or sherry

Soak the mushrooms for half an hour and drain. Remove
stems and cut caps into quarters. Rinse, soak, wash and drain
'tree-ear' fungi. Rinse hair seaweed, soak for 5 minutes and
drain. Rinse bamboo shoots, soak for 15 minutes, drain and
cut into 5-cm (2-inch) sections. Soak dried chestnuts in water
for half an hour and cut into halves. Soak lily bud stems for 5
minutes, and cut into 5-cm (2-inch) sections. Break bean-curd
sticks into 5-cm (2-inch) sections, soak in hot water for 25
minutes and drain. Soak lotus roots or gingko nuts for 15
minutes and cut into halves. Soak lotus nuts for 15 minutes
and drain. Soak bean-starch noodles for 7–8 minutes and cut
into 7.5-cm (3-inch) sections.

Cook the dried ingredients (apart from bean-starch
noodles) and fresh ingredients by stir-frying them in oil in two
separate saucepans or woks. Stir-fry for 3–3½ minutes each.
Put the ingredients together in one saucepan or wok. Pour in

the stock and stir in the soya sauce, bean curd 'cheese' and rice wine or sherry. Bring contents to boil, and simmer gently for 6–7 minutes. Add the bean-starch noodles, turn and stir, and mix evenly with the other ingredients in the pan or wok. When contents reboil, reduce heat and simmer gently for another 6–7 minutes. Sprinkle contents with sesame oil and serve.

Cold- and Hot-tossed Noodles

Cold-tossed noodles are a hot-weather dish, eaten often throughout China in the summer. They can be served with a single sauce poured over the noodles and stirred into them; or with several sauces placed on the table so that diners can help themselves to whatever sauce or sauces they would like to mix into their own bowl of noodles. Since we Chinese treat noodles as a form of bulk food like rice, to which savoury foods or sauces have to be added to make them more appealing, most of the relishes and sauces which go well with rice can also be applied to noodles (see pages 102–4). Usually, in addition to small platefuls of pickles, salted and marinated vegetables, and sauces such as mushroom, Sichuan aubergine and bamboo shoot, tomato and black bean (ratatouille chinoise), egg and butter bean, which should be provided in bowls on the table, there should be a bowlful of mixed peanut butter with sesame oil, stock and soya sauce (6 tbs peanut butter, 4 tbs salad oil, 2 tbs sesame oil, 3 tbs light soya sauce, 1 tbs red chilli oil and 3 tbs double-strained vegetarian stock), one large bowlful each of shredded cucumber, well-washed and drained bean sprouts, and one smaller bowl or dish of finely shredded ginger in aromatic vinegar. The diners should be provided with their own individual bowl of parboiled noodles. They help themselves to pinches of the relishes and spoonfuls of one or more of the sauces, which should be poured on top of the noodles, with a thin spread of bean sprouts and shredded cucumber. To add more zest to the dish, a spoonful of aromatic vinegar with shredded ginger may be scattered over it all before tossing and mixing all the ingredients together with the noodles and eating them in mouthfuls with gusto. Cold-tossed noodles served in this way can be a fascinating and inexpensive way of starting a dinner party.

Cold-tossed Noodles with Sweetened Brown-bean Sauce

Strictly speaking, this dish should be called 'warm-tossed noodles', as, except for the shredded vegetables, the ingredients could be lukewarm. The sauce is also known as Soya Jam Sauce.

To parboil the noodles, cook them in boiling water (4–5 minutes for fresh, or 7–8 minutes for dried depending upon the noodles; 14–15 minutes if using spaghetti) until barely done. The noodles should then be quickly rinsed under running water and drained. A small amount of vegetable oil (about 1½ tsp) should then be sprinkled and stirred into them to keep them from sticking. They can either be used as they are, or they can be heated up by being quickly immersed in boiling water for quarter of a minute. (575 g/1¼ lb dried noodles, and 800g/1¾ lb fresh noodles will be required for 4–5 portions.)

A bowlful of Soya Jam Sauce, or Sweetened Brown-bean Sauce (to serve 4–5) can be prepared by heating 5–6 tbs brown-bean sauce with 3–4 tbs sugar, 1½ tbs vegetable oil, 1½ tbs chopped ginger (chop into fine grains), 2 tbs soya sauce, and 300 ml (½ pint) water. Heat all the ingredients together in saucepan or wok, stirring all the time over medium heat, until the liquid has been reduced by one third or a half. The sauce obtained should be poured into a large or medium bowl and set on the table together with 3–4 other bowls containing: bean sprouts, shredded cucumber, shredded radish, egg threads (egg pancake, shredded), chopped spring onions, and chopped coriander. The first three items should be contained in large bowls, and the last two in small/medium bowls. These bowls of ingredients should also be supported by an additional small/medium bowl of 'aromatic vinegar' (or wine vinegar).

The diner sprinkles his personal bowl of noodles with 2 tbs of sauce, and lays over them a thin spread of shredded vegetables. Another tablespoon of sauce and one of vinegar are sprinkled on top of the vegetables before tossing them all together. Because of the rich sharpness of the sauce and the crunchiness of the vegetables cushioned against the firm softness of the noodles, any diner will tuck into such a bowl of noodles with considerable satisfaction.

Hot-tossed Noodles with Sesame (or Peanut Butter) Sauce

The diner sprinkles his own hot bowl of noodles with chopped spring onions, then places 2–3 tbs of peanut butter sauce on top. When the freshly chopped spring onion and sauce are stirred into the hot noodles, they generate a unique fragrance, highly appealing to both the nostrils and the palate. Like eating roasted peanuts, most people, given the opportunity, tend to eat more than they bargained for!

Serves 3–4

450 g (1 lb) dried noodles (or 700 g/1½ lb fresh)	2 tbs sesame oil
4 spring onions	3 tbs vegetable oil
5–6 tbs peanut butter	3 tbs light soya sauce
	4 tbs warm vegetarian stock

Parboil the noodles in the same manner as in the previous recipe. Heat them just before serving by immersing in boiling water for 10–12 seconds. Drain thoroughly. Divide the noodles into the personal bowls of the diners.

Finely chop the spring onions. Mix the peanut butter, sesame and vegetable oils, soya sauce and stock together until well blended. Serve the spring onion and sauce in separate bowls.

Fried Noodles or Chow Mein

Fried noodles are really parboiled noodles which have been stir-fried with a savoury stir-fried dish (in our case, a savoury stir-fried vegetable dish). 'Chow' means 'stir-fry' and 'mein' is noodles. To make a dish of chow mein, parboiled noodles are stir-fried and mixed with half the ingredients of a stir-fried dish in order to give the noodles an overall savouriness. The noodles are topped with a hot garnish made from the remaining half of the stir-fried dish. This should be given an extra stir and a turn over high heat for a minute or two in a frying pan or wok. The dish will expand in bulk quite considerably because of the noodles, so you will need to add one tablespoon each of oil and soya sauce at both stages of stir-frying. An average stir-fried dish (see pages 62–80) should be sufficient with 1 lb dried noodles, or 1½ lb fresh noodles, for 3–4 portions of fried noodles or chow mein.

Chow mein is very frequently served in restaurants, since in restaurant kitchens there are often leftover bits and pieces of raw foods which can be added to ready-cooked dishes to make excellent chow meins. When food materials are cut small and subjected to high-heat stir-frying, they release and generate flavour which can in turn be transmitted to bulk foods such as noodles, making them much more appealing and palatable.

Fried Noodles or Chow Mein with Stir-fried Mangetouts, Baby Corn, Dried Mushrooms and 'Tree-ear' Fungi

This recipe is an example of using a ready-cooked dish to prepare fried noodles or chow mein, which can be served on its own as a complete meal.
Serves 3–4

450 g (1 lb) dried noodles (or 800 g/1¾ lb fresh)	100 g (4 oz) mangetouts
	100 g (4 oz) canned baby corn
4 medium-sized dried mushrooms	2 tbs 'tree-ear' fungi
	3 tbs soya sauce
1 medium-sized onion	2 tbs dry sherry
3 tbs vegetable oil	

Prepare the noodles by parboiling them (dried noodles for 7–8 minutes, or fresh noodles for 4–5 minutes), and drain. Rinse under running water and drain thoroughly. Soak dried mushrooms in boiling water for half an hour, retaining mushroom water. Cut onion into very thin slices.

Heat 2 tbs oil in a large frying pan or wok. Add the orfion and half the stir-fried mangetouts, baby corn, mushrooms and 'tree-ear' fungi and stir over medium heat for 2 minutes. Add the noodles, spread them out over the ingredients in the pan or wok. Sprinkle them with 1½ tbs soya sauce and mushroom water, and stir-fry the noodles and the other ingredients together for 2½ minutes. Transfer the contents on to a well-heated serving dish.

Add the remaining oil into the same pan or wok. Add the balance of stir-fried mangetouts, baby corn, mushrooms and 'tree-ear' fungi to the pan. Sprinkle them with sherry and the balance of soya sauce. Stir-fry them over high heat for 1 minute. Transfer the contents and use them as garnish on top of the noodles in the serving dish. If there are any bits and pieces of fresh food which need using up, they can be sliced or chopped small and added to the pan with the onion slices at the beginning of the stir-frying to provide additional flavour.

Crispy Noodle Nests

Fried noodles or chow mein are sometimes served in 'nests'. These can be made quite easily and they make a very picturesque presentation.

The 'nests' are made by parboiling the noodles in the usual manner – dry noodles for 7–8 minutes, and fresh noodles for 3–4 minutes (noodles for this purpose can be underboiled by ½–1 minute). After the noodles have been softened by boiling, drain and spread them out evenly in one layer to cover the bottom of a metal sieve. Sprinkle the top of the still-moist noodles lightly with 1 tbs of cornflour. Spread another layer of noodles on top of the first layer, and press the top layer down with the aid of another metal sieve of about the same size as, or slightly smaller than, the first.

All that needs to be done now is to submerge the sieves with the flattened noodles in hot boiling oil for 2–3 minutes. When the noodles are golden brown and crispy, drain and remove the sieves. The noodles will be shaped like cups or 'nests' which can be used to contain and serve any stir-fried dish, providing its sauce is not too runny. To steady the 'nests' (since they all contain some sauce), it is best to place them inside a bowl before pouring the stir-fried dish into them.

Braised Mushroom Noodles with Mangetouts and Quail Eggs, Served in a Noodle Nest

This large crispy noodle nest, filled to the brim with noodles and mushrooms, and decorated with the green of the mangetouts and quail eggs, is an extremely picturesque sight and almost looks like a real bird's nest, full of food for the young and topped by a few bird's eggs!
Serves 3–4

5–6 medium-sized Chinese
  dried mushrooms
75–100 g (3–4 oz) mangetouts
2 slices root-ginger
4 quail eggs
3 tbs vegetable oil
¼ tsp salt
1 tsp sugar
1 large noodle nest (see page
  132)
100–150 g (4–5 oz) Chinese straw
  mushrooms
100–150 g (4–5 oz) French
  champignons

4–5 tbs double-strained
  vegetarian stock
1½ tbs light soya sauce
1 tbs butter
4 tbs white wine
1 pinch pepper
¾ tbs cornflour blended in 3 tbs
  water
450 g (1 lb) parboiled noodles
  (tossed with 1½ tsp vegetable
  oil to prevent noodles
  sticking)

Soak Chinese dried mushrooms in boiling water for half an hour, retaining mushroom water. Remove stems, and cut caps into quarters. Top and tail the mangetouts, and cut diagonally across the middle into two halves. Cut ginger into shreds. Boil the quail eggs for 3½ minutes and shell.

Heat oil in a frying pan or wok. When hot, add ginger and dried mushrooms. Stir them together for 1½ minutes. Add the mangetouts, salt and sugar. Pour in the retained mushroom water. Stir-fry all the ingredients together for 1 minute. Cook over medium heat for a further 2 minutes. Remove the mushrooms and mangetouts with a perforated spoon, and place half of them in the noodle nest, lining the bottom and sides.

Add the straw mushrooms and champignons to the remaining sauce in the pan or wok. When contents start to boil, add stock, soya sauce, butter, wine and pepper. When they reboil, reduce heat and cook gently for 3–4 minutes. Stir in the blended cornflour, which will thicken the sauce. Add the parboiled noodles to the sauce, and turn and stir with the rest of the ingredients in the pan or wok. When the noodles have heated through and are evenly coated with the sauce, transfer them (with a metal spoon and the help of a pair of chopsticks) to fill the noodle nest. Gradually build up the noodles and mushrooms in the nest, layer by layer, pouring the residual sauce over them, using the remaining mangetouts and dried mushrooms and quail eggs to decorate the sides and top of the noodles.

Casserole of Cooked Noodles with Four Soya-braised Chunky Vegetables, and Semi-soup Dish of Mushrooms, Pickles, Cucumber and Cabbage
Serves 4–5

To prepare this composite dish, put both the ready-cooked dishes (see pages 76 and 82) in a casserole, add 300 ml (½ pint) of vegetarian stock, 1½ tbs soya sauce and 2 tbs red or white wine and bring the contents to boil. Simmer for 5–6 minutes, then stir in 1½ tbs cornflour blended with 4 tbs of water to thicken the sauce. Once the sauce has thickened, add 1¼–1½ lb parboiled noodles to the casserole and cook gently with the other ingredients for about 3–4 minutes. Once the noodles are heated through the dish is ready to serve.

The aim is not for the noodles to be impregnated by the flavour of the sauce and other ingredients, but for them to act as a bland buffer which sets off the savouriness against the firm, satisfying texture of the noodles themselves.

Crispy Rice-flour Noodles

Crispy noodles look like vermicelli, are grey-white in colour and can be bought in 225 g (½ lb) packets. They are not served on their own, but are usually eaten with soft-fried noodles to provide a contrast of texture in the same dish. The crispy noodles form a bed on a large serving dish, and a dish of freshly cooked soft-fried noodles are spread on top. Not infrequently a portion of crispy noodles is broken up into smaller pieces and sprinkled on top of the soft-fried noodles to produce a crouton effect. Thus the soft-fried savoury noodles are served in between a bed and a layer of crispy noodles. The diner stirs and mixes together the two types of noodles with their contrasting textures, and it is this interplay of textures which intrigues the palate.

These light crispy noodles can be made very quickly as follows:

Serves 4–6

225 g (8 oz) rice-flour noodles
vegetable oil for shallow-frying
  or deep-frying 600 ml–1.2 litres
  (1–2 pints)

Divide the rice-flour noodles into 4–6 portions, so that you fry only one portion at a time (immediately after hitting hot oil, the noodles will rise and almost explode into ten or more times their original volume, into a white mass of crispy noodles).

Heat oil in a frying pan or wok. Leave over a medium heat for 1½ minutes, or until a crumb will sizzle audibly when dropped into it.

Drop rice-flour noodles into the hot oil. Remove with a large perforated spoon and place them on absorbent paper to remove any excess grease. Repeat the procedure until you have obtained the right quantity of crispy noodles. Some chefs would crush these crispy noodles before laying them out as bed for a dish of soft-fried noodles or chow mein (page 130), to be poured over them, but I prefer to spread them out lightly in a layer over a large serving dish. You can mix together the crispy and soft noodles as you eat, rather than stirring them all up together from the start.

'Liang Mein Huang' or Double-browned Noodles
Serves 4–5

These are shallow-fried (usually egg) noodles which come in pads of about 6–7.5cm (2½–3inches) in diameter. They are boiled first for 3–4 minutes, and when softened they are loosened out into a thick pancake. This noodle pancake is then fried in a frying pan in a small amount of oil (about 2–3tbs) until it begins to brown on one side. It is then turned or flipped over and fried with a bit more oil (1–1½tbs) to brown on the other side. It is then transferred to a serving dish.

Although the noodles should be brown and crispy on either side, they should still be fairly soft in between. The diner should be able to feel both the softness and the crispness of the noodles in each mouthful as he or she consumes the dish. Almost any savoury stir-fried dish with thick sauce can be used to pour over these double-browned noodles as toppings to complete the dish.

A Topping for Double-browned Noodles
Serves 4–5

4–5 Chinese dried mushrooms
2 slices root-ginger
75g (3oz) marinated bamboo
   shoots (available canned)
2 cloves garlic
2 spring onions
3½tbs vegetable oil
½tsp salt
75–100g (3–4oz) bean sprouts

3tbs green peas
4–5tbs vegetarian stock
2tbs soya sauce
½vegetarian stock cube
2½tsp cornflour blended in
   4tbs water
1tsp sesame oil
300g (12oz) double-browned
   noodles

Soak mushrooms in 150ml (¼pint) boiling water for half an hour (retain half the mushroom water). Shred ginger and bamboo shoots. Coarsely crush garlic. Cut spring onions into 1-cm (½-inch) shavings (separating the whites from greens).

Heat oil in a frying pan or wok. When hot, add mushrooms, ginger, garlic and salt. Stir-fry them for 1½ minutes over medium heat. Add whites of spring onion, bean sprouts, peas and bamboo shoots, and continue to stir-fry for 1 more minute. Add stock, mushroom water, soya sauce and crumbled stock cube. Stir and cook them together for 3 minutes. Add the spring onion greens, and stir in the blended cornflour. When the sauce thickens and becomes translucent, sprinkle the contents with sesame oil.

Pour the contents from the pan or wok over the double-browned noodles in a serving dish. Since the noodle pancake, which has been browned on both sides, is quite firm, it is helpful for Westerners who may not be able to manage with chopsticks, to cut the noodles into 5–6 pieces with a knife.

Noodle Soup

Noodle soup is as popular and as regularly served in China as chow mein or soft-fried noodles. It might even be more widely served than fried noodles in the winter, as it is a much more warming and substantial dish. Noodle soup is not quite like soup (which in China does not represent a meal on its own) because it is meant to stand on its own – as a meal on its own.

A soup can be made into a noodle soup simply by adding noodles to soup during the last stages of cooking. But, generally speaking, for a soup to qualify as noodle soup a considerable amount of noodles has to be added (roughly 75–100 g/3–4 oz cooked noodles per bowl). This greatly lowers the savouriness of the soup, since the added noodles are unseasoned. In order to maintain the savouriness of the dish, the soup will have to be pepped up with some flavouring ingredients. The most widely used are pickles, such as snow pickles, winter pickles or hot Ja Tsai pickles, in addition to dried mushrooms, dried shrimps, dried salted turnips, snow pickle or dried kelp. It is only after the adding of these ingredients that flavouring agents such as soya sauce, hoisin sauce, chilli sauce and vegetarian stock cubes can also be added to further vary the seasoning. Once the general level of the seasoning and savouriness of the soup has been raised, the cooked noodles may then be added to heat up in the soup for a short while (a few minutes), with the other ingredients before the dish can be served. Again, the reason for cooking the noodles in the soup is not so much for the noodles to absorb the flavour of the soup, but to provide a bland contrast, which will increase the appreciation of the soup itself.

However, there are soups, like Hot and Sour Soup (page 31), which, because of its high seasoning and savouriness in the first place produces a substantial and acceptable noodle soup using 100 g (4 oz) plain boiled noodles to 300 ml (½ pint) soup; but most other soups require the addition of a certain amount of dried, salted and pickled flavouring ingredients and sauces before the plain boiled noodles are added. The following recipes are examples.

Spinach and Braised Bamboo-shoot Noodle Soup

The noodle soup should be divided evenly into 4–5 large bowls to be served to individual diners. The enjoyment of consuming such a large bowl of noodle soup is the combination of tucking into the noodles, and drinking the savoury soup.

Serves 4 as a large snack or complete meal

700 g (1½ lb) cooked noodles
  (dried or fresh)
2 tbs vegetable oil
2–3 tbs snow pickle (coarsely
  chopped)

2 spring onions
4 portions Spinach and Braised
  Bamboo-shoot Soup (page
  113)
2 tbs light soya sauce

Boil dried noodles for 5–6 minutes, or fresh for 3–4 minutes, and drain. Heat oil in a saucepan or wok. When hot, add the pickles and the spring onions. Stir-fry them for 1½ minutes. Add soup and soya sauce. When contents start to boil, reduce heat and allow them to simmer together for 2 minutes. Add the noodles, stir and distribute them evenly in the soup. Cook gently for a further 2–3 minutes and the noodle soup is ready to serve.

Chinese White Cabbage Noodle Soup with Ratatouille Chinoise

This dish should not only be satisfying to consume but should also be very appealing visually.

Serves 5 as a large snack or complete meal

2 tbs vegetable oil
2 tbs snow pickle (coarsely chopped)
2–3 cloves garlic (crushed and coarsely chopped)
300 ml (½ pint) vegetarian stock
½ vegetarian stock cube

4–5 portions Chinese White Cabbage Soup (page 116)
700 g (1½ lb) cooked noodles
4–5 tbs Savoury Tomato and Black-bean Sauce or Ratatouille Chinoise (page 108)

Heat oil in a saucepan or wok. When hot, add pickle and garlic and stir-fry them together for three-quarters of a minute. Pour in the stock, and sprinkle it with crumbled stock cube. When contents boil, stir a few times , then add the soup. Reboil, and add the noodles. Allow 2–3 minutes for the noodles to heat through, and the contents to simmer together. Transfer into a large serving bowl and top with heated Ratatouille Chinoise. Allow the 4–5 diners to help themselves from the common serving bowl.

Vegetable Stem and Noodle Soup with Mushroom Sauce

Serves 4 as a large snack or complete meal

2 tbs vegetable oil
1½ tbs Ja Tsai pickle (coarsely chopped)
2 tbs snow pickle (coarsely chopped)
1 medium-sized onion (coarsely chopped)
300 ml (½ pint) vegetarian stock

½ vegetarian stock cube
4 portions Vegetable Stem Soup (page 118).
700 g (1½ lb) cooked noodles
4–5 tbs Savoury Mushroom Sauce (page 107)
2 tbs coriander leaves (chopped)

Heat oil in a saucepan or wok. When hot, add the pickles and onion, and stir them over medium heat for 2 minutes. Pour in the stock and sprinkle with crumbled stock cube. When contents boil, add the soup and the noodles. Allow 4–5 minutes for the soup and noodles to cook together.

Serve as in the previous recipe in a large communal serving bowl, topped with heated Savoury Mushroom Sauce, and sprinkled with 2 tbs of chopped coriander leaves (optional).

7 Pasta

Besides noodles, the other most important Chinese pastas are the steamed buns and dumplings. The simplest of Chinese steamed buns are the plain unstuffed *man tou*. In north China, in school dining halls and colleges, and workers' canteens, these *man tous* are provided steaming in baskets or in shallow metal buckets for the diners to help themselves from and are consumed with rice and savoury dishes which are served on the table.

In the south, however, no steamed buns are provided at mealtimes, and only rice is served. They are eaten only as snacks in between meals; and then they are generally stuffed with some fillings. Few southerners would appreciate solid steamed buns with no filling at all! Unstuffed steamed buns are really made to eat with stewed dishes, when there are gravies and sauces to be soaked up; or they are consumed with crispy dishes where the softness of the dough provides a welcome cushion to the crackling of deep-fried foods. But the southerners are more used to and appreciative of the stuffed variety of buns and dumplings which, like the Western sandwich or hamburger, are portable and convenient to eat on journeys or during picnics.

On more elaborate occasions, such as at a party or banquet, where solid steamed buns might appear too heavy and unrefined, these dough products are made into steamed 'flower rolls' and 'silver thread rolls', which, like the steamed *man tous* (or solid steamed buns), are served with stews or crispy and crackling dishes.

All this steamed pasta is made from raised dough which is prepared in the following manner.

Yeast Dough

For 450 g (1 lb) plain flour use 1 tsp dry yeast (dissolved in 2 tbs warm water). Allow 5–6 minutes for the yeast to dissolve completely. Add flour and 1 tbs sugar to a large mixing bowl and mix them well together. Make a well in the centre. Add the dissolved yeast, and pour in 200 ml (⅓ pint) lukewarm water. Stir with a wooden spoon until the flour and water are evenly mixed, and form into a large lumpy ball. Turn the ball out on to a floured surface and knead it hard for 5–6 minutes. The dough and kneading surface may have to be floured a couple of times in the process. By the end of this time the dough should have become smooth and springy. Transfer the dough into a large covered bowl or pot to stand and rise for 2 hours in a warm part of the kitchen.

After 2 hours, place the risen dough again on a lightly floured surface and flatten it with the palm of your hand. Sprinkle the surface of the dough evenly with baking powder. Fold the dough over twice and knead it again, working it hard, for a further 5–6 minutes. It should now have become smooth and firm.

Plain Solid Steamed Buns or Man Tous
Makes 8–10

Divide the yeast dough (see above) into two, and form each section into a large sausage-shaped strip about 15 cm (6 inches) long. Use your palms to help form regular-sized rolls. Use a knife to cut each roll into discs 2.5 cm (1 inch) thick. Arrange the discs on the floured surface of a tray and cover them all lightly with a cloth. Allow the dough pieces or discs about 45–50 minutes to rise, when they should have become twice their original size.

Cover a large heatproof plate or tray with a damp cloth and evenly spread out these dough pieces on top. Insert the tray or plate into a steamer, and steam vigorously for 15 minutes. Turn off the heat, and allow the steamed buns to stand for a minute or two, before removing and transferring them on to a well-heated platter.

Although these steamed buns or *man tous* are no larger than the average Western rolls, because they are quite solid few people can eat more than three or four during a meal with savoury dishes served. But they are very useful and satisfying to eat with plenty of sauce and gravy. These buns are often served with rice, and an average Chinese diner may eat a bun with a bowl or two of rice or a couple of buns with a bowl of rice. The weight-conscious Westerner would probably consume no more than half that amount.

Steamed 'Flower Rolls' or Hua Juan

For elegant people on more elaborate occasions the same dough used for plain steamed buns can be used to make the somewhat lighter 'flower rolls'.

Divide the dough into two. Roll each part into a rectangular sheet about 30 cm (12 inches) long and 20 cm (8 inches) wide. Brush the top of each sheet with 1 tbs sesame oil. Roll the dough sheets lengthwise firmly into the shape of swiss rolls about 4 cm (1½ inches) in diameter. Cut each roll crosswise into lengths of approximately 10 cm (4 inches).

Place one roll on top of another, and press them together lightly. Use a chopstick to press down heavily across the centre of the two rolls. This will cause the ends of the top roll to lift or open up (and on steaming the edges of both top and bottom rolls will open up further, making them look like the petals of a flower). Continue until you have made a dozen of these 'flower rolls'. Line them up on a floured surface, and cover them with a dry cloth. Leave them to stand for about three-quarters of an hour by which time they should have doubled their original size.

These 'flower rolls' should be steamed vigorously in the same manner as the plain steamed buns, on top of a heatproof plate covered with a damp cloth, for about 15 minutes. Although these rolls weigh the same as the plain steamed buns, they look much lighter than the more solid buns. They are seldom eaten with rice (rice is not served during Chinese banquets, where there are often as many as a dozen courses of savoury dishes) and therefore serve the purpose of counteracting the over-savouriness of a lengthy multicourse meal.

'Silver Thread' Steamed Rolls

These are considered to be even more refined than the steamed 'flower roll' buns in the previous recipe. These are also made by rolling out half the yeast dough into a thin rectangular sheet 30 × 20 cm (12 × 8 inches). Cut the sheet into halves across the longer side. Divide one of the halves into two sheets for use as 'wrappers'. Brush the surface of the other half lightly with a small amount of sesame oil, and fold it over. Use a sharp knife to cut this folded sheet of dough into matchstick-thin strips. Take two strips up at a time with your fingers and pull them gently until they are about 15 cm (6 inches) long. When you have finished cutting and pulling these dough strips into 'dough threads', divide them up into two lots. Roll and wrap them up tightly in the dough wrappers provided, tucking in the ends and allowing the weight of the roll to rest on the edge of the wrapper (the latter will cause the wrapper to seal during steaming). Allow these wrapped-up 'silver thread' rolls to stand on greaseproof paper and rise for three-quarters of an hour. When ready, arrange them on a heatproof plate, cover with a damp cloth, and steam vigorously for 20 minutes. Turn the heat off and allow them to stand in the steamer for 2 minutes, before removing.

As these 'silver thread' steamed rolls are over 15 cm (6 inches) long they will need to be cut with a sharp knife into 3–4 slices across the dough threads on serving. Being made up of these innumerable 'threads', these rolls absorb even more sauce or gravy than the average plain steamed buns, or 'flower rolls'. Hence they are often used at parties and banquets, in conjunction with stewed and long-braised foods, to add a measure of refinement to what might otherwise appear to be informal dishes.

Stuffed Steamed Buns

These stuffed buns are probably one of the most popular and portable snacks of all Chinese food. They are 'self-contained' (each bun contains both the bulk food and the savoury fillings), they can be conveniently carried, and they can be eaten hot or cold (like sandwiches). But, above all, they are pleasant to eat (the slight touch of sweetness in the dough contrasting with the savoury saltiness of the fillings seems to add to their appeal). Using the same yeast dough as on page 142, they are quite simple to make. The fillings, however, will need to be cooked briefly first, and then allowed to cool (preferably completely) before they are stuffed into the dough, as the heating of the buns during steaming may not be sufficient to cook the fillings.

Makes 12 buns

For the stuffing:
100 g (4 oz) Chinese white cabbage
50 g (2 oz) braised bamboo shoots (available canned)
spring onion
2 tbs vegetable oil
2 tbs snow pickle (coarsely chopped)

1½ tbs Sichuan hot Ja Tsai pickle (coarsely chopped)
1½ tbs soya sauce
½ tsp sugar
1 tbs sesame oil
2 tbs watercress (coarsely chopped) or coriander leaves (optional)

Cut cabbage into 1-cm (½-inch) slices, braised bamboo shoots into shreds (cut shreds again into 1-cm/½-inch sections) and spring onion into 6-mm (¼-inch) sections.

Heat vegetable oil in a small frying pan or wok. When hot, add the pickles and braised bamboo shoots. Stir them over medium heat for 1 minute. Add the cabbage and continue to stir-fry for 2½ minutes. Add soya sauce, sugar, sesame oil, spring onion and watercress or coriander. Stir-fry them all together for a further 1½ minutes. Transfer them into a glass basin or bowl to cool. When cold, put in the refrigerator to cool further for 1½ hours.

Divide the dough into two. Roll each half into sausage-shaped rolls, 25–27.5 cm (10–11 inches) long. Cut each roll into discs approximately 2.5 cm (1 inch) thick. Flatten the discs with your palm and press them into pancakes 10–12 cm (4–5 inches) in diameter, making them slightly thicker in the centre than the rim.

Place a heaped tablespoon of the filling at the centre of each thick pancake. Lift and flute the sides of the pancake firmly around the filling, pucker and gather the rim up to cover the filling completely. When the rims meet at the top, close it off by giving them a twirl and twist, and finally a pinch. Place these buns, puckered and twisted side down, on greaseproof paper in a warm spot for three-quarters of an hour.

Turn the risen buns over and arrange them on top of a large heatproof plate covered with a damp cloth. Insert the plate and contents into a steamer and steam vigorously for 20 minutes. Allow the buns to stand for a couple of minutes before removing from the steamer. These buns can be eaten hot (preferably) or cold. When cold they can be reheated by placing them in a steamer for 6–7 minutes.

Stuffed Dumplings

In China dumplings are seldom served as solid pellets of dough as they often are in the West; they are almost invariably prepared and cooked as stuffed dumplings. These consist of savoury fillings which are wrapped in dough sheets, made by mixing flour with hot water (if the dumplings are meant to be steamed) or cold water (if they are meant to be boiled). The usual proportion for 18–24 dumplings is to mix one portion (or cup) of water to 2½ portions of all-purpose flour.

To prepare the dough wrappers, first place the flour in a large mixing bowl. Make a well in the centre and add water very gradually. Start by adding just one third of the water and stir to make a firm dry dough. Add more water slowly and continue to stir until the two ingredients are thoroughly mixed. It is important to add water gradually, as more water can always be added as you go along. Knead the dough in the bowl for 3–4 minutes, and leave it to stand for 20 minutes to allow the dough to rise. Turn the dough out on a lightly floured surface, and knead for another 5 minutes. Divide the dough into two portions. Rest one portion in the bowl, and cover with a damp cloth. Make the other half into a large sausage-shaped roll about 30 cm (12 inches) long. Cut the roll into a dozen discs 2.5 cm (1 inch) thick. Use your hand and palm to flatten the disc, and roll each one with a small rolling pin into a pancake wrapper approximately 6 cm (2½ inches) diameter and 3 mm (⅛ inch) thick. Give the pancake a quarter turn each time you roll, to keep it as round in shape as possible. This is the wrapper with which to wrap the fillings.

Place a tablespoon of filling in the centre of the pancake. Turn down and fold over the top two-fifths of the wrapper to barely cover the filling. Bring up the lower edge of the dough, pleating it slightly as you do so, and pinching the two edges together with thumb and finger to close and seal the dumpling. Repeat the process until all the dumplings are made. Arrange them on a floured tray, while you wait to bring 1.75–2.25 litres (3–4 pints) water to boil in a large saucepan.

There are three ways in which these dumplings are cooked: they can be *water-boiled, steamed* or *half boiled and half shallow-fried.*

Most common is the 'water-boiling' method. Put the dumplings in the large pan of boiling water and cover. When contents reboil pour in a cup or a small bowl of cold water. Replace the lid and wait for the contents to boil again. When this happens remove the lid and pour in another cup of cold water. Repeat this procedure three times, after which the dumplings should be cooked and normally float up to the top. Remove them with a perforated spoon.

These boiled dumplings are normally served with three types of dip sauces (soya sauce, chilli oil or chilli sauce, and shredded ginger in vinegar) which are placed on the table for the diners to dip their dumplings in. These simple dumplings are often eaten as bulk food in north China, and people think nothing of eating twenty to thirty of them at a meal at a time, but in the south they are eaten in much smaller quantities as snacks.

These dumplings can also be steamed by arranging them on top of a large heatproof plate covered with a damp cloth, and steaming them vigorously for 18–20 minutes.

The third way of cooking these dumplings, which is peculiar to Beijin is quite unique, and is to part boil, and part fry the dumplings. The usual way of doing this is to heat a heavy frying pan or skillet over high heat. When very hot add 3–3½ tbs oil to heat in the pan for 30 seconds. Swirl the oil around until the surface of the pan or skillet is evenly greased. Reduce heat to medium-low. Add all the dumplings, crowding them together; tilt the pan so that its sides and the sides of the outer dumplings are well greased. Add 2 tbs oil to a cup of boiling water. Stir them together and pour them evenly over the dumplings. The contents will start boiling and frothing. Shake the pan so that any dumpling which is slightly stuck to the side or bottom will loosen. Cover the pan with a lid, and leave contents to cook steadily for 5–6 minutes. Uncover the lid, shake the dumplings and see how much water there is still in the pan. Raise the heat to allow the water to evaporate more quickly. Once the water has almost completely evaporated turn off the heat altogether. Use a spatula or fish slice to remove the dumplings. Arrange them on a well-heated dish and serve them with same dip sauces as for the boiled dumplings. They are a great source of satisfaction to all those who appreciate Peking cuisine.

Griddle Cakes

The two most popular are onion cakes (or spring onion cakes) and sesame cakes. These are simple to make and although very much a food of the masses, many Chinese regard them with nostalgia.

Onion (or Spring Onion) Cakes

These onion cakes are enjoyable to eat both because of their aromatic quality, and because of their slight saltiness. They are usually eaten on their own, but of course they also go very well with savoury foods, especially crunchy stir-fried vegetable dishes.
Makes 10

450g (1 lb) all-purpose flour	2 tsp coarse-grain sea salt
¼ tsp baking powder	5 spring onions (coarsely
½ tsp sugar	chopped)
150 ml (¼ pint) warm water	5–6 tbs vegetable oil

Place flour in a mixing bowl. Sprinkle evenly with baking powder and sugar. Mix with a wooden spoon. Add water gradually, stir and mix with the wooden spoon. Knead the dough with your hand and palm for 3–4 minutes. Cover with a damp cloth, and leave for half an hour. Then knead again for 2–3 minutes. Divide the dough into ten portions and form into narrow strips 20–25 cm (8–10 inches) long. Flatten the strips with a rolling pin into ten flat dough bands of pancake thickness. Sprinkle each band first with salt, and then with chopped spring onions. Roll the bands lengthwise into long double-thickness spaghetti-shaped strips. Hold one end of the strip and turn the other end around in circles until the concentric rings form themselves around the centre into a spiral pancake. Flatten the 'pancake' with the palm of the hand. Repeat until the dough has been made into ten spiral pancakes.

Heat the oil on the bottom of a large flat-bottomed frying pan. When hot, lift the handle of the frying pan so that the surface of the pan is evenly greased. Place the spiral pancakes on the surface of the pan. Fry over low heat for 2½–3 minutes, and turn the pancakes over. Repeat and fry gently until the pancakes are evenly browned on either side.

Sesame Cakes

These sesame cakes can be eaten on their own, or they can be served with savoury foods. They are made from the same dough as is used for the onion cakes in the previous recipe, except that no sugar and only half the salt is added. The dough is simply divided into ten portions, and padded into round cakes 4mm (⅙inch) thick. The top of the cake is then pressed on to a trayful of sesame seeds leaving each one thickly covered. These cakes are then heated, seed side down, on the hot surface of a dry griddle until they are well browned and toasted. They are then turned over to heat on the other side of the hot griddle. For best results, they should be put into a preheated oven to bake for another 2–3 minutes at 80°C/350°F (gas mark 4) before serving.

Spring Rolls

Spring rolls, or egg rolls as they are also often called in America, are one of the most commonly served items of food in Chinese restaurants in the West. The wrappers for these crispy pancakes are best bought, as they are widely available from Chinese foodstores and supermarkets, in packs of 50 sheets at a time. They can be stored for a considerable length of time in the refrigerator. There remains therefore only the filling which needs to be cooked.

Filling for Spring Rolls
Makes 15–20

6–7 large Chinese dried
  mushrooms
3 spring onions
3½ tbs vegetable oil

2 slices root-ginger (shredded)
75g (3oz) celery (shredded)
50g (2oz) young carrots
  (shredded)

1 tsp salt
1 tsp sugar
a pinch of pepper
75 g (3 oz) bean sprouts

1 tbs light soya sauce
3 tsp cornflour blended in 2 tbs
water

Soak mushrooms in boiling water for half an hour. Remove stems and cut caps into shreds. Cut spring onions into 2.5-cm (1-inch) sections.

Heat oil in a frying pan or wok. When hot add mushrooms, ginger, celery and carrots. Stir-fry them over high heat for 2½ minutes. Add salt, sugar and pepper, and continue to stir-fry for 1 minute. Add sprouts and soya sauce and stir for a further 1½ minutes. Add blended cornflour and stir until all the vegetables are well coated by the sauce and more than half of the liquid has evaporated. Remove contents and place them in a bowl to cool. When completely cold the filling will be ready to use to stuff the pancakes.

The pancake wrappers are square-shaped dough sheets measuring about 10 × 10 cm (4 × 4 inches) square. Place 2 tbs of the cooked filling along a line for about 6 cm (2½ inches) across the middle of the wrapper (between two corners). Bring up the bottom corner and fold over to cover the filling, and then bring in the corners from the two sides, which should nearly meet in the middle. Finally, bring down the top corner and roll the package over into a firm roll (like a large sausage roll) and close by wetting the last corner with a small amount of beaten egg. Rest the pancake roll on top of the last corner, while you stuff the remaining rolls.

Deep-fry the pancake rolls in moderately hot oil for 6–7 minutes, or until golden brown and crispy. They can be eaten with or without dip sauces (such as soya or soya and chilli) but they must be consumed hot and crispy.

Self-filled Spring Rolls

These spring rolls are seldom eaten in the West but are served in China to welcome the advent of spring. They are not fried spring rolls but simply plain water-and-flour pancakes which are heated on a griddle for 2–3 minutes either side and are used to wrap round a collection of quick-fried shredded vegetables. These vegetables can vary in number from two or three to half a dozen. They are just lightly quick-fried so that they retain most of their crispiness and are used in conjunction with two or three, or more, dip sauces. The following are typical vegetables used in these rolls, and the quantities given should be sufficient to stuff 20–30.

75–100 g (3–4 oz) bean sprouts
2 tbs root-ginger (finely shredded)
4 tbs vegetable oil
1 tsp salt
1½ tbs light soya sauce
75–100 g (3–4 oz) Chinese white cabbage (shredded)
2 tbs Ja Tsai pickles (finely shredded)

1 tbs yellow bean sauce
75–100 g (3–4 oz) celery (shredded)
75–100 g (3–4 oz) firm button mushrooms
75–100 g (3–4 oz) young carrots (shredded)
1 tbs sesame oil

The bean sprouts and ginger should be stir-fried together over high heat for 1½ minutes with one third of the seasonings. The same applies to the shredded cabbage and Ja Tsai pickle. The remaining oil, seasonings and sauce should be used to stir-fry the celery, mushrooms and carrots for about 2½ minutes. These three separately stir-fried collections of vegetables should be contained in separate serving dishes, and grouped at the centre of the dining table for the diners to stuff and fill their own pancakes. Dishes or small bowls of dip sauces should also be provided and should consist of good quality soya sauce, chilli sauce, vinegar with shredded root-ginger, and yellow bean sauce with sugar and sesame oil (mix together 4 tbs yellow bean sauce, 2 tbs sugar, 1 tbs vegetable oil, ½ tbs sesame oil and 3 tbs water, and stir over a moderate heat in a small saucepan for 3–4 minutes until consistent).

8 Fruit, nuts and flowers

Although fruits are eaten widely in China, we do not necessarily end our meals with a sweet dessert. Sweet dishes, however, are often used as side dishes, or pauses, to provide variations in the long march of a multicourse Chinese meal, during which a diner may feel almost overwhelmed by the continuation of hot savouriness, despite its subtle nuances and variations, and the occasional interjection of a fresh, pure, fruity, refreshing sensation is often very welcome.

On the other hand, there are also fruit soups and fruit gruels, sweet nut soups and bean soups, which are drunk, like hot cocoa, for warmth and comfort. Many such items are combined and constituted dishes in which the inherent flexibility of Chinese food preparation comes into full play. This enables almost any number of dishes to be created – along the lines of the dried with the fresh, the juicy with the nutty, the sweet with the less sweet, and so on. The majority of these, especially the drier dishes, can be garnished or decorated with flowers.

Partly because of the frequent presence of sweetness in a large number of savoury dishes, sweet-tasting fruits with a firm texture, such as apple, pear, melon and pineapple, can often be cut into the same shape and size as the principal ingredient and incorporated into stir-fried or quick-braised dishes without disturbing their character; or in some cases they may be incorporated in the longer cooked soya-braised dishes by adding them to the pot or pan during the later stages of cooking. For instance, shredded pears can be mixed into most hot-tossed and cold-tossed noodles (page 128–30), or into Stir-fried Bean Sprouts with Spring Onions (page 65); and apples can easily be incorporated into most hot and sour or sweet and sour dishes. Chunkily cut apples can be incorporated and cooked in a dish of Four Soya-braised Chunky Vegetables with Pickles (page 76), or even into a dish of Sichuan Hot-braised Stir-fried Aubergine (page 77). Many palates find the combination of sweet and hot an appealing sensation and flavour. But it is when fresh fruits are cut into small pieces and combined with nuts and dried fruits in a basic food material such as rice that the greatest range of dishes begins to emerge. The Chinese cookery custom of combining the sweet with the salty and savoury makes it particularly exciting.

Sweet Fried Rice with Cherries

This dish is only mildly sweet and can be eaten with other salty and savoury dishes. The large mound of fried rice, studded with red cherries and speckled with the greens of spring onion, looks very attractive and is also very appealing to many palates.
Serves 4–5

2 spring onions	450g (1lb) cooked rice
1–2 salt eggs	½tsp salt
1 medium-sized onion	1tbs sugar
7–8 medium-sized cherries	1½tbs light soya sauce
2–3 eggs	2tbs vegetarian stock
4tbs vegetable oil	1tbs butter or margarine
3tsp capers	
4–5tbs sweet corn kernels (available canned)	

Chop spring onions into 4-mm (⅙-inch) shavings (separating the whites from greens). Rougly chop the salt eggs and onion. Remove the stones from cherries. Beat the eggs lightly.

Heat 3tbs oil in a frying pan or wok. When hot, add onion and whites of spring onion. Stir them in the hot oil for 1½ minutes. Add salt egg and capers, continue to stir for one minute, then push them to one side of the pan or wok. Add remaining tablespoon of oil to other side of the pan, and pour in the beaten egg. When the eggs are about to set, add the sweet corn. When the eggs have completely set, reduce heat and scramble the contents together. When they are well mixed, push them to the side. Pour the cooked rice into the centre, and stir and mix it in with all the other ingredients. Sprinkle with salt, sugar, soya sauce and stock. Continue to turn and stir until all the ingredients are well mixed into each other. Add butter or margarine, the spring onion greens and cherries, and toss together with the other ingredients. Leave to cook over low heat for 1 more minute. Turn the contents out on to a large, well-heated serving dish.

Fried Rice with Braised Bamboo Shoots, Braised Carrots, Green Peas and Salted Peanuts with Violets and Nasturtiums
An uncommonly attractive dish, which is equally satisfying to consume.
Serves 4–5

1 medium-sized onion	3 eggs
2 spring onions	4–5 tbs miniature tomatoes
75 g (3 oz) braised bamboo shoots (available canned)	4 tbs vegetable oil
	450 g (1 lb) cooked rice
75 g (3 oz) braised carrots	4–5 tbs green peas
2 tbs soya sauce	1 tbs butter
½ tbs sugar	½ handful of violet and
2 tbs snow pickle	nasturtium petals

Cut onion into very thin slices, spring onions into 4-mm (⅙-inch) shavings and bamboo shoots and carrots into 5-mm (⅕-inch) pieces (braise carrots by heating the sliced carrots in 1½ tbs oil for 1½ minutes, add 2 tbs soya sauce and ½ tbs sugar, heat gently for 3 minutes and drain). Coarsely chop snow pickle and spring onion. Lightly beat eggs in a bowl. Cut tomatoes into halves.

Heat 3 tbs oil in a frying pan or wok. When hot, add onion and stir it for 1½ minutes. Add bamboo shoots and continue to stir for 1 minute. Then push them to one side of the pan or wok. Add oil to the other side of the pan or wok, followed by the eggs. Reduce heat to allow the eggs to set slowly. When the eggs have set, scramble them with the other ingredients, and push them to the sides of the pan or wok. Pour the rice into the centre. Bring in the ingredients from the sides and scramble them together with the rice. Allow contents to cook gently for 1 minute. Add tomatoes, braised carrots, peas, butter and chopped snow pickle. Sprinkle with spring onion. Continue to stir, turn and mix all the ingredients together. Leave contents to cook for a further minute.

Transfer the contents from the pan or wok into a mound on a well-heated serving dish. Sprinkle and surround it with violets and nasturtiums, and serve.

Fried Rice with Peanuts, Radishes, Diced Pressed Bean Curd, Sultanas, Soya Eggs, Apples and Jasmine Buds

This large, grand mixture of fried rice, representing a wide variety of textures, flavours and colours, is a substantial dish for anyone with an appetite to tuck into. It should also be an attractive dish to present at a dinner party. Although sugar is added, it is not quite a sweet dish for it contains quite an element of saltiness. It could be described as a 'sweet and salt' dish!
Serves 4–5

1 medium-sized onion	1 tsp salt
2 soya eggs	450 g (1 lb) cooked rice
50–75 g (2–3 oz) seasoned pressed bean curd	2 tbs sultanas
1 medium-sized red apple	1½ tbs butter
3 eggs	3 tbs green peas
4 tbs small radishes	2 tsp sugar
4 tbs vegetable oil	2 tbs light soya sauce
3 tbs salted peanuts	½ handful jasmine buds
	1 tsp sesame oil

Cut onion into very thin slices. Cut soya eggs and pressed bean curd into 5-mm (⅕-inch) cubes. Dice apple (including skin) into 6-mm (¼-inch) cubes. Beat eggs lightly. Coarsely chop radishes.

Heat 3 tbs oil in a frying pan or wok. When hot, add onion

and stir-fry for 1 minute. Add peanuts, pressed bean curd, radish and salt. Stir-fry them together for 2 minutes, and push them to one side of the pan or wok. Add remaining oil to the other side of the pan. After quarter of a minute pour in the beaten egg. Reduce heat and wait until the eggs have set completely before scrambling them with all the other ingredients. Push the scrambled ingredients to the sides of the pan or wok. Pour the rice into the centre, gradually bring in the ingredients from the sides to stir, and mix evenly with the rice. Leave contents to cook over low heat for 1 minute. Add sultanas, butter, peas, soya eggs and apple. Sprinkle them with sugar and soya sauce. Turn and toss them together until all the ingredients are evenly mixed.

Turn the contents out on to a large serving dish, piling them all up in one mound. Sprinkle them with a handful of jasmine buds and sesame oil, and serve.

Chinese Rice Gruels, Rice Puddings and Sweet Soups

The following recipes illustrate the central point which rice oocupies in Chinese food, whether sweet or savoury, vegetarian or otherwise. Many of these rice dishes, sweetened and cooked with fruits, etc., have probably evolved through convenience. Since rice is readily available in the Chinese kitchen, and is neutral in taste, it can go together just as well with sweet ingredients and fruits as with meats, vegetables and savouries. 'Sweet soups' occur frequently in the lengthy sequence of a multicourse Chinese dinner and are used to 'punctuate' the run of several savoury dishes. They are thought to have a cleansing and refreshing effect on the palate, before embarking on the second or third leg of savoury dishes (which a Chinese banquet or party dinner may well offer).

Lotus Nuts and Orange Tea

This is one of the favourite sweet soups (here the word 'tea', which is commonly used in China, is taken to mean 'sweet soup'). The nutty,

sesame taste of the dumplings provides a contrast to the more general sweet orange taste of the soup.
Serves 6–8

337 g (12 oz) canned lotus nuts

900 ml (1½ pints) water

3–4 tbs sugar

6 oranges

2–3 tbs sweet candied (glacé) ginger

1½ tbs sesame paste or peanut butter

4–5 tbs rice flour

2 tbs cornflour blended in 5 tbs water

Drain the lotus nuts. Place them in a clean saucepan and add water and sugar. Bring to the boil, and reduce heat to a simmer. Continue to cook gently for 15 minutes. Meanwhile, peel the oranges, squeeze the juice from 3 oranges, and chop the remaining oranges into 6-mm (¼-inch) pieces. Chop ginger into coarse grains. Add sesame paste or peanut butter and 2½ tbs water to the rice flour in a mixing bowl. Mix and mash them together into a thick dough paste. Form the paste into 12–15 small dough balls or dumplings.

Put the dumplings into the saucepan in which the lotus nuts are simmering. When contents reboil, add the orange juice, chopped oranges and ginger. Stir, and when contents have reboiled again stir in the blended cornflour, which should thicken the soup. Cook for a further 1–2 minutes.

The 'tea' or sweet soup should be poured into a large serving bowl, then ladled out into small individual bowls for the diners to sip from – in small mouthfuls, as it is likely to be very hot.

Sweet Rice Gruel with Prunes and Pears
As with most of these soups with a high sugar content, this is inclined to be very hot.
Serves 7–8

175–200 g (6–7 oz) glutinous rice

2 litres (3½ pints) water

5 tbs sugar

225 g (8 oz) canned prunes

3 medium-sized pears

3 tbs candied orange peel

Prepare the gruel first. Boil the rice in water, reduce heat to very low, and simmer for 1½ hours. Add the sugar, prunes and prune syrup. Peel and score the pears and cut them into 1-cm (½-inch) pieces. Rougly chop orange peel. When the contents reboil, add the pears and peel and cook gently for a further 15 minutes.

Serve as in the previous recipe in small individual bowls, to be sipped and eaten slowly.

Sweet Rice Gruel with Lotus Nuts and Chinese Red Dates
Serves 7–8

225 g (8 oz) Chinese red dates
175–200 g (6–7 oz) glutinous rice
2 litres (3½ pints) water
5 tbs sugar

225 g (8 oz) canned lotus nuts
2–3 tbs candied ginger (roughly chopped)

Bring dates to boil in a small saucepan of water and simmer gently for 35 minutes. Drain, pip and chop the dates, cutting each one into quarters.

Prepare the rice gruel as in the previous recipe. When ready, add the dates and sugar and simmer together for 15 minutes. Add drained lotus nuts and continue to simmer for a further 10 minutes. Serve to the diners individually in small bowls, to be sipped and eaten slowly.

Sweet Rice Gruel with Fruit and Nuts
Serves 6–7

3–4 tbs dried figs
2–3 tbs candied ginger
1½ tbs sultanas
1½ tbs raisins
6 medium-sized strawberries
2 slices pineapple

1–1.2 litres (1¾–2 pints) rice gruel (see page 99)
4–5 tbs sugar
4–5 tbs almonds or walnuts (coarsely chopped)

Chop figs and ginger to the same size as the sultanas. Cut strawberries into halves, and pineapple into 1-cm (½-inch) wedges.

Heat rice gruel in a large saucepan. Add pineapple pieces, figs, sugar, sultanas, raisins and nuts. Bring contents to boil, and simmer gently for 25 minutes. Add the strawberries and simmer for 5 minutes. Serve in the same manner as the two previous recipes.

Sweet Peanut Soup with Strawberries or Cherries
Serves 5–6

1.5 litres (2½ pints) water
1½ tsp baking powder
350 g (12 oz) raw peanuts
1 tbs butter
4–5 tbs sugar

1½ tbs cornflour blended in
  4 tbs water
225 g (8 oz) small, fresh
  strawberries or cherries

Heat water in an enamel saucepan. When warm, stir in the baking powder. Add the peanuts and bring contents to boil. Reduce heat, cover and simmer gently for 1½ hours. Remove lid and simmer for a further half an hour. Add butter and stir in the sugar and cornflour. Stir until they have completely dissolved.

Remove the stalks from the strawberries or stone the cherries and add to the pan. Turn contents around and simmer for a couple more minutes.

Serve in individual small bowls as a 'break' in a sequence of savoury dishes.

Sweet Lotus-nut Soup with Cherries
Serves 5–6

1.2 litres (2 pints) water
1 tsp baking powder
300 g (10 oz) canned lotus nuts
1½ tbs cornflour blended in
  4 tbs water

4–5 tbs sugar
1 tbs butter
225 g (8 oz) large cherries

Heat water in an enamel saucepan. When warm, stir in the baking powder. Drain the lotus nuts and add them to the pan. Bring contents to boil, and simmer gently for 1 hour. Add cornflour, sugar and butter. Stir until they have completely dissolved and the soup has thickened.

Remove the stalks and stone the cherries. Place 4–5 cherries at the bottom of each small serving bowl, and pour in the sweetened lotus-nut soup. Serve one bowl to each diner, either to conclude a meal or in the course of it to break the sequence of savoury dishes.

Sweet Ginger Soup with Dried Lichees
Serves 5–6

900 ml (1½ pints) water
4–5 tbs fresh root-ginger
 (skinned and shredded)
225 g (8 oz) dried lichees

4–5 tbs candied ginger
3–4 tbs sugar
1 tbs cornflour blended in 3 tbs
 water

Heat water in an enamel saucepan. Add ginger and bring to boil. Reduce heat and simmer for half an hour. Remove the ginger with a perforated spoon. Remove the shells of the dried lichees and add them to the pan to simmer for half an hour. Chop ginger glacé into quarter-sugar-lump-sized pieces, and add them with the sugar to the pan. Stir in the blended cornflour, which will thicken the soup.

Serve in small bowls to the individual diners. Small rose petals may be sprinkled on top of each bowl of soup to add colour.

Sweet Green Pea Soup with Lichees
Serve 5–6

450 g (1 lb) dried green split
 peas
900 ml (1½ pints) water
450 ml (¾ pint) rice gruel (page
 99)

4 tbs sugar
225 g (8 oz) canned lichees

Soak peas in water overnight. Bring to boil in the same water. Simmer gently for 1½ hours. Add the rice gruel and stir in the sugar. Gently bring to boil, and continue for a further 20 minutes. Add the lichees, including syrup, and bring to the boil once more. Stir, then serve by ladling into small bowls for individual diners, as in the previous recipes.

Sweet Red-bean Soup with Fresh Loongnan (or Dragon Eye) Fruit
During the summer loongnan are grown and harvested in south
China in greater profusion than lichees. They are therefore used
extensively in numerous forms of sweet dishes.
Serves 5–6

350 g (12 oz) dried red beans
900 ml (1½ pints) water
450 ml (¾ pint) rice gruel (page
 99)

4–5 tbs sugar
350 g (12 oz) fresh or canned
 loongnan (dragon eye)

Soak beans in water overnight. Bring them to boil in the same
water. Simmer gently for 1¼ hours, uncovered. Add the rice
gruel and stir in the sugar. Gently bring to the boil and
continue to simmer for a further 15 minutes. Add the shelled
or skinned loongnan (including syrup if canned). Bring once
more to a gentle boil. Stir and simmer for 10 minutes.

   Serve by ladling into small individual bowls, as in the
previous recipes.

Baked Apples Stuffed with Red-bean Paste
Serves 6

15 tbs red-bean paste: see below
 (or canned from Chinese
 foodstores)

6 medium-sized apples

Sweet red-bean paste can be made as follows: soak 450 g (1 lb)
dried red beans overnight in 1.2 litres (2 pints) water. Bring
the water and beans to boil in a deep casserole or enamel
saucepan. Reduce heat and simmer gently, uncovered, for 2
hours until most of the water has evaporated. Put the softened
beans and remaining water through a blender to make a
consistent paste. Return the paste to the casserole or saucepan
and stir over low heat until the beans become much drier
(about 20–30 minutes). Slowly add 4 tbs sugar and 6 tbs
vegetable oil, and continue to stir all the time to prevent
burning. After 20 minutes, remove from the heat and allow the
sweetened bean paste to cool. When cold, the bean paste
should be ready for use as a filling to stuff the apples.

Cut a 1-cm (½-inch) slice horizontally off the top of each apple (retain the slice to use as a lid). Core the apples, but leave a wall 8mm (⅓ inch) thick all around and at the base, excavating some of the pulp. Fill two-thirds of the cavity with the bean paste. Close the top of the cavity with the sliced apple-top. Secure it by inserting a toothpick.

Fill a roasting pan with 2 inches of water. Preheat the oven to 190°C/375°F (gas mark 5). Stand the apples in the water and insert the roasting pan into the oven to bake for 30 minutes. The apples should have become quite tender and pleasant to eat in mouthfuls with the sweet filling.

Peking Dust

Peking Dust was a very popular dessert in Peking in the 1920s and 30s, especially enjoyed by Western communities, who were enjoying their heyday in China's ancient capital.
Serves 4–5

450–600g (1–1¼lb) chestnuts	300ml (½pint) double cream
½tsp salt	2tbs castor sugar
3–4tbs sugar	a sprig rose bud with 1–2 leaves

Score chestnuts with a criss-cross cut on the flat side of each piece. Add to boiling water and cook for three-quarters of an hour. Drain and shell the chestnuts. Grind the chestnut meat in a blender into a powder, fold and blend in the salt and sugar. Whip the cream and fold and blend in the castor sugar.

Divide the chestnut mix into 4–5 portions and pile each one into a mound at the centre of 4–5 small dessert plates. Top the mounds with 2–3tbs sugared whipped cream. Place a sprig of rose bud at the base of each mound of Peking Dust, half buried by it, as if it were a solitary bloom which is surviving unattended and uncared for in a corner of a desert!

Glazed Honey Bananas or Apples

The unusual sensation of crackling through the thin coating of crystallized sugar (like thin ice) which is highly sweet, and chewing and munching it with the softer ingredient of fried banana or apple underneath, makes this a delicious dish. For a decade now this has

been one of the favourite desserts served in Pekingese restaurants in the West. The attraction of the dish can be further enhanced by serving these pieces of apple or banana encased in a sweet crystallized coating in conjunction with scoops of different coloured fruit sorbets, strewn with the petals of different coloured flowers.
Serves 4–6

4 medium-sized bananas or 3 medium-sized apples	*Syrup*: 7–8 tbs sugar
3 tbs cornflour	5–6 tbs water
1 egg (lightly beaten)	3 tbs honey
oil for deep-frying	3 tbs vegetable oil

Cut bananas into quarter-length segments (or cut apples into quarters, and further cut each quarter into halves). Sprinkle and rub with cornflour, and wet with beaten egg.

Deep-fry the banana or apple pieces until slightly brown. Remove and drain on absorbent paper.

Meanwhile, prepare the syrup by mixing and heating the syrup ingredients together in a small saucepan over medium heat, stirring all the time until the mixture begins to turn brown. Dip the fried banana or apple pieces into the syrup of molten and somewhat caramellized sugar and coat. Retrieve the banana or apple pieces with the aid of a pair of chopsticks, and dip them quickly into a bowl of iced water. Remove immediately and drain on the greased surface of a platter. The sudden dip into iced water crystallizes the coating, which will crack when bitten into.

When a sufficient number of banana or apple pieces have been dipped, crystallized and drained, arrange them on a serving dish for the diners to help themselves.

Harvest 'Eight-Treasure' Rice Pudding

This is a classic Chinese dessert which is frequently served during any Chinese dinner party or banquet. By surrounding the pudding with chrysanthemums, which begin to bloom during the early autumn, it gives the added feeling of gaiety associated with the time and season of harvesting.
Serves 8–10

3 tbs butter or margarine
5–6 tbs coloured glacé fruit
2 tbs sultanas
2 tbs raisins
350 g (12 oz) glutinous rice
4 tbs sugar

2 tbs vegetable oil
300 ml (½ pint) sweetened red-
bean paste (page 99)
5–6 tbs nuts: lotus nuts, melon
seed meat, peanuts

Rub the sides and bottom of a heatproof bowl or basin generously with butter or margarine. Press on the glacé fruit, sultanas and raisins in an artistic pattern so that they stick on to the walls and base.

Prepare the rice by washing and boiling it in 1¼ times its own volume of water over very low heat for 15 minutes and leaving it to stand for a further ten minutes. Stir in the sugar and oil and mix evenly with the rice. Spread a layer 2.5 cm (1 inch) thick of rice evenly over the bottom and sides of the bowl or basin, completely covering the glacé fruit, sultanas and raisins (taking care not to knock any of them off). Spread a layer 1 cm (½ inch) thick of red-bean paste over the rice on the bottom of the bowl. Add another layer of rice 2.5 cm (1 inch) thick to cover the bean paste. Sprinkle the top of the rice with the nuts and the meat of melon seeds, then cover these with 1 cm (½ inch) of rice. Repeat the procedure, until there are three seams of bean paste, rice, nuts and melon seeds, ending up with a thick layer of rice, which should come to within 1 cm (½ inch) of the brim of the bowl or basin. Cover firmly with foil.

Insert bowl or basin with its contents into a steamer for 50–60 minutes. Turn the contents out on to a large round serving dish in a swift inverting action (the edge of the pudding may be loosened first by carefully inserting the blade of a knife all round). This Chinese Eight-Treasure Rice Pudding should sit on the serving dish rather like a Christmas pudding, except it is very much more colourful. It can be made even more colourful by surrounding it at the base with small blooms of chrysanthemum, thus endowing it with an even more festive atmosphere of harvest time!

Index